AF429868

Life Under Divine Influence

God's Truth About Law and Grace

Stephanie M. White

Copyright © 2020 by Stephanie M. White

ISBN: 9798638950149

All rights reserved. No part of this book may be reproduced or transmitted in any form or by any means, electronic or mechanical, including photocopying, recording, or by any information storage and retrieval system, without permission in writing from the copyright owner.

This book was printed in the United States of America.

To order additional copies of this book, contact:

https://whitestephanie83.wixsite.com/heavenonearthforyou

Introduction

Romans 6:23 KJV
For the wages of sin is death;
but the gift of God is eternal life
through Jesus Christ our Lord.

Law and grace have long been debated by those who have a knowledge of God's Word. This debate is futile for those who do not know Christ, however. We can have knowledge of the Word and not know Jesus Christ as Savior. If we do not have a personal relationship with Christ, then our studying is in vain.

The Word of God is not a textbook; it is not a history book. It is true that it does include educational and historical facts, but the Word of God is His love letter to us. It is a book of life for those who know Jesus Christ as their personal Savior. If you do not know Jesus Christ as Savior, this is your opportunity to receive the gift of eternal life.

God is presenting you with a gift. A gift cannot be earned or deserved; a gift must be received. Eternal life is

God's gift to you. What is eternal life? Eternal life is life that is perpetual, it is continuous and never-ending; eternal life is Spiritual life. Eternal life is living in the presence of our loving Savior. Eternal life is a gift given through Jesus Christ. He took the wages of our sin upon Himself because we couldn't pay the price for our sins. This gift is given freely; all we have to do is receive it. The thief on the cross received it by faith. He simply turned to Jesus and articulated his faith in his own words and Christ received him with open arms (Luke 23:42-43). We can do the same. Jesus is not looking for the perfect prayer or the perfect performance. He is not willing that any should perish but that all should have eternal life. Turn to Him if you haven't already. Speak your faith in what He has done for you.

Jesus Christ tasted death, Spiritual death, so we could avoid it. Spiritual death is separation from God and thanks to our Savior, we will never experience this separation if we receive Christ's gift of forgiveness and eternal life. This does not mean that we will never experience a natural or physical death here on earth. As we leave this earth for our heavenly home, this death is the doorway. Natural or physical death is not to be feared; therefore, it is no longer a threat to those who are in Christ.

God's gift of eternal life begins the day we receive it and it will never end. Our physical bodies will see an end, but our Spirit never will.   Eternal life (or Spiritual life) can be experienced here on earth. The Bible tells us that God's will should be done on earth as it is in heaven (Matthew 6:10). What God has planned for us in heaven can begin to be experienced here on earth. We can experience the gift of Spiritual life here and now by abiding in the Word. The more we fill ourselves with the Word the more we will experience life as it is in heaven, or Spiritual life, here on earth.

As we take in God's Word, a work is being done in us. His Word is transforming us and it is enabling us to participate in our Spiritual nature - His nature.

As you read this book you will be encouraged to focus on the eternal, on Jesus Christ rather than self. As our focus on Him grows, so will the harvest of Spiritual fruit in our lives. He will increase and we will decrease and life will be better than we could have ever imagined.

Chapter 1

A LONG STORY SHORT

Romans 7:10 NIV

I found that the very commandment that was intended to bring life actually brought death.

As a child of God I longed to live as God intended. I am sure you are familiar with this desire as well. We go to church, we read God's Word, we pray, we fast, and so much more, in our attempt to discover His plan for living life. Our attempts lead us to believe that this plan is elusive and must be miraculously and painstakingly discovered, but God was very clear when He instructed us on His plan for life. God's plan has always been the same and it has always been simple and it has always been distinctly presented.   God's plan is for man to depend on and live through His Word. Man's distorted view of this plan has caused much confusion, however, and it has put the spotlight on man rather than God. Man's plan has even been incorrectly labeled as Christianity by some. We must know the difference.

What is the law and what was God's plan where the law was concerned? Is the law the opposite of grace? Paul refers to the law (or the commandment) as something that was intended to bring life. In the original Greek translation of this verse, the text reads that the commandment actually *was* life – not merely intended to bring life, but life itself. We also see that the word that was translated as "commandment" is the word for a prescription. A prescription is a proven formula for a desired effect: God's prescription for man is His Word and it will produce Spiritual life (Deuteronomy 32:47). Life is found in His Word. We see this reiterated throughout the Scriptures. The law, the commandment, the prescription, or the Word of God, is the proven method for living life as God intended. The Word is our Spiritual life.

Seeing that this is God's plan, we must ask, "What happened?" How did that which was given as life come to be perceived as death? As we continue on in the seventh chapter of Romans, we see that the commandment, or the prescription, taught what sin was and it gave man the power to defeat sin. As man became aware of what sin was we also find that sin became man's center of attention rather than the Word. Man's preoccupation with sin gave sin the upper hand. The Word was perceived as death when the sinful acts became the focus of man instead of the Word of God.

Whenever man looks at the Word of God as a rulebook rather than a life-giving love letter, death ensues. God furnished us with His Word to enable us to live a godly life; it was never given as a challenge to live holy. God's intention was never for man to attempt to live up to the Word; man was always meant to live *through* the Word.

Exodus 19:5-6 KJV Now therefore, if ye will obey My voice indeed, and keep My covenant, then ye shall be a peculiar treasure unto Me above all people: for all the earth [is] Mine: And ye shall be unto Me a kingdom of priests, and an holy nation. These [are] the words which thou shalt speak unto the children of Israel.

We see that God instructs the children of Israel to obey His voice and to keep His covenant prior to the giving of what we refer to as the Ten Commandments. God's plan for man was to obey His voice and to keep His covenant. What exactly does this mean?

In order for us to clearly understand what God is saying, we must go back to the Hebrew translation of God's Word. As we look at the phrase, "obey His voice indeed," we see that it is translated from the Hebrew words, *shama shama qol*. The word *qol* is simply defined as voice in the Hebrew;

the word *shama*, however, is far more interesting. This Hebrew word is an intimate description of how we should connect with the Word of God (or His voice). In its definition we find many facets: intelligent and attentive hearing, careful gathering and collecting, contentment, the ability to speak intelligently, the ability to understand and the ability to obey the Word (or see the Word manifested in our lives). This Hebrew word reveals God's plan for man.

The Hebrew word *shama* draws attention to the fact that we should be attentive to the Word of God and we should intelligently hear what God is saying to us. Hearing intelligently requires studying. God refers to those who study the Word as disciples. Disciples are those who continue in the Word and learn the truth of the Word; as a result, they experience the freedom of the Word (John 8:31-32 KJV). Studying the Word requires time. It is a consistent intake of the Word that produces faith (Romans 10:17). We cannot ignore the Word and expect to experience all that God has promised.

A disciple gathers the Word. They study verse after verse. They look for more than one verse that proves God's point – they look for reproof. Many times we look at the word "reproof" and assume that it means correction or criticism, but it can also mean to prove again or evidence. God's Word is profitable for reproof (2 Timothy 3:16 KJV). It proves itself over and over again; it is the only evidence you require. As a disciple, or one who follows God's plan to *shama* His Word, you will collect God's Word on a subject and see that God is faithful. He gives proof and reproof that His promises are valid. The Word will always be proven faithful; therefore, we can rest content in His promises without any further proof. Contentment is a result of His Word being our focus.

The Word of God will produce faith as we consistently ingest it (Romans 10:17). This faith will produce Spiritual fruit in our lives. The Spiritual fruit of our lips is such an example: we believe and as a result we speak (2 Corinthians 4:13). Jesus also told us that out of the abundance of our hearts our mouths would speak (Matthew 12:34). As we take in the Word, the Word becomes part of who we are. Faith is produced and that faith produces the ability to intelligently speak in agreement with the Word; this is another facet of the Hebrew word *shama*.

In the definition of *shama* we also find that it involves understanding. As we unite with Christ, we are in a state of understanding. Understanding has to do with seeing ourselves in Christ and we cannot do that without the Word. The Word of God teaches us who we are in Christ; it opens our eyes to who we are as His Bride. We must see ourselves in Christ –

the two become one. When we *shama* His voice we are hearing Him as the love of our lives. We know who we are in Christ – our identity is found in Him and not in ourselves. The Word of God was intended to bring life, but it will bring death when we are self-centered rather than Christ-centered. As a child of God, we must see ourselves as God sees us. We must read the Word as a dearly loved child of God, a joint-heir with Christ.

Finally, we find that the definition of *shama* includes the ability to obey. This is the word that *shama* is usually translated as. When we study the definition for *shama* and its various facets, I find it interesting that this is the word that man chose to use as the English translation for this intimate word. This selection puts the focus on man rather than on God. This word, rather than any of the others in the definition of *shama*, makes man's specious ability the focal point. Again, this word makes us self-centered rather than Christ-centered. The use of the word "obey" implies that if man could just conform and be good enough, then everything would be fine and God would be pleased. This is not what God is saying. Our ability to obey (or see the Word manifested in our lives) is found in our decision to fill ourselves with the Word and thus witness faith and the fruit faith produces in our lives.

To obey or follow the Word is nothing more than the Spiritual manifestation of a heart that is full of the Word. Faith is what produces Spiritual fruit – period!

Faith is what pleases God because He is the Source of Spiritual faith (Hebrews 11:6). Spiritual faith is the victory that overcomes this world and all that it encompasses (1 John 5:4). We overcome our flesh by the Spirit (Galatians 5:16). Apart from Jesus Christ we are Spiritually bankrupt.

"*Shama shama qol*" – God used the Hebrew word *shama* twice when He instructed us regarding His voice; the depiction of *shama* was that important. He wanted us to recognize our desperate need for His Word. This word describes how we are to regard the Word in our lives - we are to see it as our very life. It shows us that we must require the Word as a vital necessity if we want to live out His Word in our daily lives.

We are also told to "keep His covenant" in several Scriptures. The word that "keep" was translated from is the Hebrew word *shamar*. *Shamar* also describes a personal and dependent relationship with the Word – or His covenant (Psalm 105:8). *Shamar* refers to hedging the Word in; it refers to guarding the Word and protecting it in your life. This word describes the job of a watchman. The watchman, in Biblical times, was to guard what he was protecting with his life. In using this word, God is revealing to us the worth and value of His Word; He is telling us that the Word is worth guarding with our lives. If we reject the Word in our lives, we are rejecting Spiritual life. The Word *is* our Spiritual life!

The Word of God is your Spiritual life! Jesus told us that the words He speaks are Spirit and they are life (John 6:63). We must fill ourselves with His Word in order to live a Spiritual life. As we begin to understand what the Word truly is, we will begin to guard it with our lives. It will become precious to us - something we cannot live without.

Shamar also describes vision; it is defined as looking narrowly. The Word of God is supposed to be our focus. That is God's plan for man. It always has been and it always will be. He truly is the same yesterday, today, and forever.

Our vision needs to be single. We need to be focused solely on the Word. Our flesh provides us with many distractions, however. As a child of God, we must understand what is vital and what it futile. For example, it is futile for us to try to pay for our sins or waste time succumbing to the distraction of feeling guilty for our sins. The payment Christ paid for us to be free from sin and to be declared innocent in His sight was accepted by the Father and it is imperative that we rest in that truth. There will always be thoughts and ideas that contradict the Word, but we must remain intently focused on what God has said. We must fight these distracting lies with the truth of the Word.

Patience is also an aspect of the definition of *shamar*. When we are focused on the Word, when we are protecting it in our lives, we are also waiting on God. We are told that faith and patience bring God's promises to pass (Hebrews 6:12). Faith will produce patience. If we will consistently fill ourselves with the Word, then faith will be produced and that faith will produce the patience that we require (Isaiah 26:8). Our lack of patience is an indicator – it is warning us that we are low on the Word of God. When you feel like you are running low on patience, simply fill up with the Word of God. Trust the Word to do its job in your life. You cannot make yourself patient – but God can! Thank God for His Word and all that it does in our lives.

To *shama* and *shamar* the Word is to cling to the Word, to know and understand your desperate need for the Word. It is to consistently gather it in your life and keep it as your focus. It is to guard it intently as your source of Spiritual life. To *shama* and *shamar* the Word is to be totally dependent on God rather than self. It is to put God first. It is to be Christ-centered rather than self-centered.

*   *   *

When God instructed the children of Israel regarding His Word, He began by instructing them to keep Him first.

Deuteronomy 5:7 NIV You shall have no other gods before Me.

The phrase, "You shall have," was translated from one Hebrew word which means to follow and to require. God instructed them to follow Him and to require Him. God must be first. We must require Him in our lives above all. An idol is *anything* that takes the place that belongs to God in your life – *anything* that comes before Him. We can even become our own idol. I know I have struggled with the expectations that I have placed on myself and it took my focus off of Christ and put it solely on me. I became so focused on me that there wasn't any room in my life for God. I thought I was being godly by trying to be good enough and trying to modify my behavior, but I was simply absorbed with self - I was indulging my flesh and I didn't even know it. We must recognize the consequence of being self-centered or self-absorbed: we become our own idol.

We must understand that God needs to be our priority. When God is our priority, the Word is our priority because He is the Word and He will always give us a passion for His

Word. As we begin to focus more and more on the Word, He begins to increase and we begin to decrease. Our attention to the Word takes our attention away from self - it does this as long as we read the Word as our Spiritual Seed rather than a list of rules and regulations we must try to live up to.

In the following verses we see a list of "thou shall nots" – this phrase was also translated from one Hebrew word. It is the Hebrew word for no, never, and unable to. In the Hebrew language, we see a beautiful depiction of God's plan for man that we miss in the English translation. According to God's plan, if we will first require Him in our lives as our Source, then (as a result) we will not make any graven images and bow down to them, we will not be able to use God's name in vain or for our own gratification, and so on. In God's plan, we depend on Him by following His plan to *shama* and *shamar* His Word and He then works through us by transforming us into His image. He keeps us from sin because we cannot keep ourselves from it. What an amazing God!

Galatians 5:16 NIV So I say, live by the Spirit, and you will not gratify the desires of the sinful nature.

Living by the Spirit is living a life that is under Divine influence. It is walking in agreement with the Word (Amos

3:3); it is walking by faith or living by every word that proceeds from the mouth of God (Deuteronomy 8:3). This simply means that we are following God's plan to *shama* and *shamar* His Word. We are requiring it in our lives, it is our priority, we are focused on it, we are protecting it, and we are filling ourselves with it; consequently, life-changing faith is being produced in our lives. When we are in agreement with His Word our lives will display that harmony. As we live as God intended, we *will* produce Spiritual fruit. We cannot walk in the Holy Spirit of God and sin at the same time; it is not possible. The Word of God will transform us just as God said it would. The Word does not come back void.

God gave man His Word as living oracles (Acts 7:38 KJV); the utterances or words of God are alive and they impart Spiritual life to those who receive them as God planned, but when we receive them as rules and regulations, they become death to us.

God presented the children of Israel with these living oracles, but they had their own perception of His Word.

Deuteronomy 5:27 NIV Go near and listen to all that the LORD our God says. Then tell us whatever the LORD our God tells you. We will listen and obey.

Man's response to the giving of living oracles was not a personal response. They wanted someone else to listen for them. Their plan included being told what to do and it included performance. The word translated as "obey" in this verse is not *shama*; it is the Hebrew word *asah*. This word means to perform or accomplish. They received the Word as a challenge or something they could attempt to live up to. They did not receive the Word as living oracles. Their decision to view the Word of God as a rulebook rather than life was not God's plan for man, but God does gives man free will.

Deuteronomy 5:28-29 KJV And the LORD heard the voice of your words, when ye spake unto me; and the LORD said unto me, I have heard the voice of the words of this people, which they have spoken unto thee: they have well said all that they have spoken. O that there were such an heart in them, that they would fear Me, and keep all My commandments always, that it might be well with them, and with their children forever!

God heard what their reaction to His plan was. The NIV translation includes the sentence, "Everything they said was good." This English sentence leads us to believe that God is happy with their decision to perform or try to live up to the Word.   The very next sentence portrays something else, however, as does the Hebrew translation. As you study out the sentence, "Everything they said was good," you find the King James makes the meaning clear by translating the original Hebrew more closely: "…they have well said all that they have spoken."

God told Moses that they clearly stated their plan – "they have well said" - they were clear that they wanted to perform the Word and keep God at a distance. They did not want God to work through them by their dependence on His Word. They wanted to do *for* God. He then goes on to say, "Oh, that their hearts would be inclined to fear Me and keep all My commands always, so that it might go well with them and their children forever!" God is not in agreement with their decision. He wants them to fear Him – to live in awe of who He is and what He does, to keep Him first. He wants them to "keep" – He wants them to *shamar* the Word so that it will go well with them and their family.

> Malachi 2:5 NIV   My covenant was with him, a covenant of life and peace, and I gave them to him; this called for reverence and he revered Me and stood in awe of My name.

God's plan for man was for man to live through Him, to live dependent on Him, and this plan or covenant would produce life, peace, and reverence. Man would live in awe of God when they lived dependent on Him and they would have peace and they would produce Spiritual fruit through the life-giving Seed of the Word.

Their rejection of God's plan to live through His Word did not agree with God's plan, but it was their choice and God will not force His will on anyone (Acts 14:6).

Romans 10:3-4 NLT For they don't understand God's way of making people right with Himself. Refusing to accept God's way, they cling to their own way of getting right with God by trying to keep the law. For Christ has already accomplished the purpose for which the law was given. As a result, all who believe in Him are made right with God.

Their hearts were more inclined to performance. They did not accept God's way of being made right with God so they came up with their own vain attempt. The word translated as understand in verse three is a Greek word that also means to ignore. They chose to ignore God's way and make their own - and God let them have their way. He does the same with us. We have our right to choose, but we must remember that our choices have consequences. We can choose Spiritual life through His Word or we can choose a carnal, lifeless existence through works of the flesh (Deuteronomy 30:19). The ways of our flesh will never bring about the good life that God has planned for us.

As we continue to dig deeper and deeper into God's Word we will find that His plan for us to live through His Word will make our lives better and bring His promises to pass for us and for our families. God's plan for man is good; man's carnal idea of God's plan is not, however.

Chapter 2

The Purpose of the Law

Galatians 3:24-25 KJV

Wherefore the law was our schoolmaster [to bring us] unto Christ, that we might be justified by faith. But after that faith is come, we are no longer under a schoolmaster.

God presented *His* plan for man to depend on His Word; nonetheless, man chose *their* plan to depend on self. Once man chose his own effort over God's, the law took new shape. God presented His Word originally as living oracles – as His very own utterances that would impart Spiritual life. Man instead regarded His Word as a challenge; so *to them*, the Word *became* rules and regulations (Isaiah 28:9-13). The very words of life became death because man was self-centered rather than Christ-centered. "*We* will listen and *we* will perform!" was the prideful reply of man. God then began to reveal man's inability to perform or achieve apart from Him.

The law was to be their schoolmaster. This word was translated from the Greek word for a servant whose office it was to take the children to school. Leadership is another characterization for this Greek word. In studying this word, we find that the law should teach us of our desperate need for Christ and lead us only to Him. It should never lead us to self-effort or pride.

Romans 10:3-4 KJV For they being ignorant of God's righteousness, and going about to establish their own righteousness, have not submitted themselves unto the righteousness of God. For Christ is the end of the law for righteousness to every one that believeth.

The law was to be a schoolmaster to lead us to Christ. When the law was not received as God intended, it then took on a new identity. As you continue reading in the Old Testament, you see that the law increased in number and severity. Why did man continue to believe that they could perform or accomplish all of this on their own? I often wonder why they did not throw up their hands and say, "We cannot possibly do all of this!" That is, in fact, the very thing that God was waiting for man to acknowledge. He wanted them to look at the law and see their desperate need for a

Savior. God did not want them to try to earn righteousness; He wanted them to receive the gift of righteousness. He wanted mankind to understand that Christ was the end of trying to achieve and deserve something from God.

The Word of God (Old Testament and New Testament) has always testified to our need for a Savior and God's gift of righteousness. The law was never given as a challenge or as a test of man's righteousness (unfortunately, it is many times received that way). The Word tells us that no one is righteous apart from Christ (Romans 3:10). **We can only *receive* righteousness; we can never *achieve* it.** God wants us to see our need for a Savior and accept Christ. We continually see this articulated in the Word of God.

In the book of Matthew, for example, chapter nineteen and verse sixteen, we see a young man come to Jesus with a question. The young man wants to know what *he* has to do to *earn* eternal life.

He wants to perform and accomplish that which can only be done by Christ. How many times are we guilty of the same? How many times do we want to produce Spiritual fruit apart from Him? Every time we try in our own effort, apart from dependence on Him and His Word, we are doing the same thing and it is foolish. To be foolish is to be acting apart from God rather than letting Him work through you; your flesh is foolish.

Jesus begins to deal with the young man. He uses the law as a schoolmaster in hopes of leading the young man to Himself. Jesus lists some of the facets of the law and the man boastfully proclaims that *he* has accomplished it all. Jesus then takes the law to the next step. This young man believed that he was a good keeper of the law, so Jesus gave him a new law – one that was personal to him.

The young man was rich – not only was he rich, but he was in love with his prosperity. He had his god that no other gods were before and it was his wealth. This young man could not walk in the Spirit because he never made God his priority. The young man had to give away all that he had because it was taking the place that only God should occupy in his life. God was not first, money was.

Jesus presented a new law to show this young man his need for a Savior; nonetheless, this young man walked away without Christ because money was his god. Money was the thing that was above all in his life. We cannot serve God and mammon – and mammon is not only wealth; it is also defined as materialism and self-reliance. Mammon is confidence and pride in anything other than God; it is what you value above Him.

Jeremiah 48:7 NIV Since you trust in your deeds and riches, you too will be taken captive…

The young man could have cried out and declared his inability to be good enough, but he did not. Our faith in anything other than Jesus Christ will lead us into a life of captivity. We will never find true freedom outside of Christ. Our trust can be in what we have or in what we do – either way, it is misplaced and will end disastrously. That is why Paul said he considered everything outside of Christ as loss (Philippians 3:7-8).

The law is to be a schoolmaster – it is supposed to show our need for God, not encourage us to believe that God wants us to conquer it by being good enough on our own. The law's purpose is to show us how lost in sin we truly are (Romans 5:20) and point us to Jesus Christ - the end of the law (Romans 10:4).   Once man decided to ignore the true purpose of the law and view it as rules and regulations (instead of living oracles), performance and self-effort prevailed.

Galatians 3:12 NIV The law is not based on faith; on the contrary, "The man who does these things will live by them."

The law (when viewed as rules and regulations) is not based on faith; it is based on what *you* do – works. Seeing the Word as rules and regulations takes the focus off of Christ and puts it on self. The man who lives his life by the law is living by what he does – not what Christ has done for him.

Many will argue that living up to the law is God's plan and that Jesus even said for us to do so.

Matthew 5:17 KJV   Think not that I am come to destroy the law, or the prophets: I am not come to destroy, but to fulfill.

This verse, like so many others, can be misunderstood. As we look at God's Word, it is imperative that we study the roots of His Word. The word "fulfill" was translated from a Greek word that is defined as to finish, to accomplish, and to execute. Christ came to fulfill – He has accomplished the law. What does that mean?

He has accomplished the law for us and we can now walk in His accomplishment by following His original plan to *shama* and *shamar* His Word. As we *shama* and *shamar* the Word, what we take in will be displayed in our lives in the form of actions, thoughts, words, and so on. His Word

alone is the Seed that will produce the Spiritual fruit we need in our lives.

He accomplished the law *for us* because it was not possible for us to do so on our own. Our vain attempts to achieve the impossible will no longer distract us when we realize this. It is finished and it was finished by the only One who could do it for us!

We cannot execute or perform the law without Him, but we can benefit from His execution and we can see Spiritual fruit in our lives through Him.

Romans 8:3-4 NKJV For what the law could not do in that it was weak through the flesh, God did by sending His own Son in the likeness of sinful flesh, on account of sin: He condemned sin in the flesh, that the righteous requirement of the law might be fulfilled in us who do not walk according to the flesh but according to the Spirit.

Christ's sacrifice was enough. The righteous requirement of the law has been met *for* us because of what *Christ* has done! We could never meet the requirement on our own because our flesh is weak. We no longer have to look at the Word as something we must live up to – Christ accomplished that for us. It is finished! We are now alive in Him and He is the end of trying to earn righteousness by our works.

We must view the Word as our Source of Spiritual life. We must see it as a mirror instead of an aspiration. The Word shows us who we already are in Jesus Christ, not who we should attempt to be. As we study the Word, we will begin to see who we already are because of Christ and this new revelation will begin to transform us into what we see in the mirror of His Word.

As we study the law and its purpose, we see that God's living oracles were never the problem; it was man's perception of them.

Romans 7:7 NIV What shall we say, then? Is the law sin? Certainly not! Indeed I would not have known what sin was except through the law. For I would not have known what coveting really was if the law had not said, "Do not covet."

As we look at the Word, we must see "Do not covet," as a promise rather than a challenge. He is not simply listing sin after sin that man must attempt to avoid –He is providing us with what we need to overcome sin and he is giving us a picture of what that looks like. We must look at all of God's instructions as promises. They are a depiction of who we are in Christ. If we will *shama* and *shamar* the Word, then we will see the manifestation of the Word in our lives. The Word is our prescription for a Spiritual life. That is God's promise! If we walk in the Spirit, we will *not* give in to the flesh. We will not have to force ourselves to refrain from covetous behavior when Christ is at work in us. Christ is in us and He provides us with the ability to avoid covetous behavior when we follow God's plan to depend on Him. He will bring about the Spiritual fruit of contentment in us as we focus on Him and abide in His Word.

Romans 3:31 KJV Do we then make void the law through faith? God forbid: yea, we establish the law.

When we live according to God's plan to *shama* and *shamar* the Word, faith will be produced. Faith will establish the Word in our lives because faith will manifest the Word in our lives. Spiritual faith *will* produce Spiritual fruit in our lives. We cannot live by faith and make His Word void at the same time – He forbade that from ever happening!

As our focus remains on Christ, He continues to work through us. His Word produces Spiritual actions, Spiritual words, Spiritual thoughts, and the like – *we* do not!   The law is established in our lives *as* we walk by faith.   Again, it is imperative that we remember what it means to walk by faith. Faith is accomplished or produced in us only as the result of our consistent intake of the Word (Romans 10:17) – and we must be taking the Word in as the source of Spiritual life that it is, not as rules and regulations.

We must regard the Word as living oracles rather than rules and regulations. We cannot perform the Word; the Word must be worked out of us by faith. And faith is not a decision that we make – we do not simply decide to believe God. Faith is the result of following the plan of God – *shama* and *shamar* the living Word.

Spiritual faith will never disagree with the Word of God; it will never transgress the Word. If the Word teaches us to avoid covetous behavior, then the Word will produce generosity and contentment in us when we walk by faith. We cannot walk by faith and sin at the same time.   In understanding this, we also understand that man's theory of "a license to sin" is a lie. We will never be in agreement with sin if we are truly walking by faith. **Faith will always establish the Word in our lives; it is our source of victory over sin.**

Many ignore or reject the Word because they see it as a challenge rather than their source of victory. Viewing the

Word as rules and regulations will defeat you. Either you will feel hopeless and give up because you cannot live up to it, or you will begin to feel prideful because you erroneously believe that you can live up to it. Either way, the focus is on you and not on God. Jesus Christ must be our focus. We must view the Word of God correctly.

God's Word has been perverted by man. To pervert is to use something in a way other than the way it was intended to be used. The life-giving Word of God has been used by man to manipulate, to guilt, to control, and to make afraid, to list a few, but it is time for us to agree with man's ways no longer. God designed His Word to bring Spiritual life – life as He has it - it is time for us to get in agreement with Him. The purpose of the law, or the Word of God, was life. The Word is not a list of rules for us to attempt to live up to; the Word is the Seed for Godly life. We cannot repeat this enough. It is His beautiful, loving, life-giving covenant with man that we need to be in agreement with.

Chapter 3

What is the Covenant?

Psalms 105:8 NIV

He remembers His covenant forever, the Word He commanded, for a thousand generations.

God sent man His Word; His Word is His covenant with man. A covenant is defined as a compact, a confederacy. It is an agreement to form an alliance or relationship. The Word is the Covenant and the Word is Jesus Christ (Revelation 19:13). Jesus Christ unites man with God. As we begin to see the Word as God sees it and depend on the Word by abiding in it, we become intimate with God. This personal relationship transforms us. We begin to think as He thinks, we begin to talk as He talks, and so on – we begin to live in agreement with God or participate in our Divine nature. In Hebrew, the word translated as "covenant" comes from a word that means to feed. This depiction emphasizes our need to feed on or ingest the Word of God. The Word is our Spiritual food; it is our Spiritual fuel. The ingestion of the Word will transform us – we are what we eat!

As we study God's covenant with man we find that it is based on His love for man. God's love for us has given us everything we need for life here on earth and our eternal home in heaven (2 Peter 1:3). His covenant of love is His Word; it is our Spiritual Source.

> Nehemiah 1:5 NIV Then I said: "O LORD, God of heaven, the great and awesome God, who keeps His covenant of love with those who love Him and obey His commands."

God's covenant is a covenant of love. He loves us so much that He sent His Son – and His Son is the Word (John 1:14). His love is His covenant; the Word is His love letter to us. We must recognize what love truly is. In many Scriptures we are told to love God, but we must bear in mind that we are also told that we can *only* love Him because He first loved us (1 John 4:19). We are tempted to put the cart before the horse, but we must reject that temptation through the truth of the Word. We need God in order to be able to love. We must not be confused when it comes to love. We cannot love apart from Him. He must always be our focus. When He is put first in our lives, love will be the result.

1 John 4:10 NIV This is love: not that we loved God, but that He loved us and sent His Son as an atoning sacrifice for our sins.

What is love? It is not our love for God; it is His love for us! His love for you is preeminent.

We must recognize that true love is *not* based on man. We cannot love God on our own. We will never be able to truly love God, others or ourselves, unless we receive His love first. True love is the love of God; it is the love that sent Christ to be the sacrifice for our sins. God is love. He keeps His covenant of love with those who love Him because He first loved them!

He also keeps His covenant of love with those who obey His commands – in this Scripture the word "obey" is translated from the Hebrew word *shamar*. Again, this word describes an intimate, dependent relationship with the Word. The covenant is the Word – in order for us to experience our covenant with God, we must be focused on the Word consistently. His covenant of love is enjoyed by those who abide in the Word, by those who live out the definition of *shamar*.

His covenant is full of promises for those who are in Christ. His covenant is a covenant of blessings that will never be broken (Isaiah 54:10 NLT). We are told that we have been blessed with every Spiritual blessing in the heavenly realms (Ephesians 1:3) – this means that the blessings are all Spiritual and that means that they can only be experienced if we are walking in the Spirit. We must be where the blessings are if we want to experience them.   God's directive to live dependent on the Word is for our good. It is exactly where we need to be.

If we are not in agreement with the Word (not living by faith, not walking in the Spirit), then we will not see the Word manifested in our lives. Faith brings about the promises of God (the Spiritual blessings) – and faith is the result of our consistent ingestion of the Word.   We cannot earn God's promises. This also cannot be repeated enough. We cannot be good enough; we cannot achieve the promises of God – if we could, then the promises would have been given in vain (Romans 4:14). There are people who believe that God will keep His end of the agreement only if they love Him enough and are good enough and that belief leads to living a lie.

> Galatians 2:16 NKJV   Knowing that a man is not justified by the works of the law but by faith in Jesus Christ…for by the works of the law no flesh shall be justified.

We cannot be justified by works – we cannot be rendered innocent as the result of our labor. It is only by faith in Jesus Christ that we can find freedom and forgiveness. God sent His Son to achieve what we could not achieve, to pay a price that we could not pay. He sent Christ because He loves us so much! **God is not depending on man's righteousness so why do we?**

> Isaiah 42:6 AMP I the Lord have called You [the Messiah] for a righteous purpose and in righteousness; I will take You by the hand and will keep You; I will give You for a covenant to the people, for a light to the nations…

Jesus Christ is our covenant; He is the Word; He is love. Again, we must perceive the covenant correctly. If we view the covenant as rules that must be kept, then we will never live as God intended.

He is my covenant. *He* has accomplished the law for me. I can do what the Word says because *He* lives in me! His Word is full of His promises to me – promises for my behavior, my thoughts, my words, my family, my career, and so much more. Each promise finds its manifestation in my life through faith and patience – it is never because of works; **the**

effort of man can never achieve what God has freely provided. That is why genuine faith cannot be weakened by our shortcomings (Romans 4:16, 19).

In Romans, chapter four, we see that Abraham could hope against hope because He was living by grace through faith. His body may have been as good as dead and his wife barren, but that could not stop God! Abraham was counting on God, not himself, and that is why he could hope against hope. He knew his God was the God of the impossible. He knew that even though his situation was as good as dead, his God was a resurrecting, life-giving God. When we are trusting in Him instead of self, we too will hope against hope because our God is not a man that He should lie - He will do what He has promised even when it seems impossible!

God's desire was to establish a covenant with man whereby *He* empowered them. God knows man – He created us. He knows who we are (Psalm 78:38-39). He knows that we cannot attain our own righteousness. God never asked man to do what man could not do; but as we have discovered, man's pride caused us to believe that we could.

Jeremiah 32:38-40 NIV They will be My people, and I will be their God. I will give them singleness of heart and action, so that they will always fear Me for their own good and the good of their children after them. I will make an everlasting covenant with them: I will never stop doing good to them, and I will inspire them to fear Me, so that they will never turn away from Me.

In God's description of His everlasting covenant, *He* is doing the work. He is giving us singleness of heart and action. He is doing good to us. He is inspiring us to fear Him and to remain focused on Him. How is He doing all of these? He is working through His Word. In the King James Version, singleness of heart and action are translated as one heart and one way. One heart – our Spiritual nature. One way – Jesus Christ. We only experience the goodness of God through Christ – He is our covenant of love and blessings that cannot be broken!

God's desire was to establish a covenant with man whereby *He* empowered them; however, man wanted to be the source of his own power. God did not ignore mankind's decision. He gave them what they wanted. God will never force His will on man; He always gives man freedom of choice. Will you choose to view the Word as a rulebook or a love letter?

Chapter 4

Do You See What I See?

Hosea 8:12 KJV

I have written to him the great things of My law, [but] they were counted as a strange thing.

For many years I viewed the Word as a rule book and I was deceived. My life was not Spiritual and I was miserable. We must view the Word correctly. Our flesh will tempt us to see it as something it was never intended to be, but through Christ we can overcome this counterfeit perception.

We must ask ourselves if we see the Word for what it truly is or if we regard it as "a strange thing" in our lives. What does it mean to count the Word as a strange thing? This phrase comes from one Hebrew word and the definition for this word includes committing adultery. It is also defined as turning aside, to be a foreigner, and to profane. God is describing people that turn aside from His truth and choose their own idea of truth. They "cheat" on the Word of God with their own customs, ideas, philosophies, and such. As

Jesus said, they set aside the Word of God in order to observe their own man-made traditions or laws (Mark 7:9).

How do you see the Word of God? Do you set it aside in order to cling to your own beliefs or something that you have been taught for years? I know I have. There were many times I thought that my traditional beliefs agreed with the Word of God only to find out that they did not. I remember boldly quoting, "God helps those who help themselves!" and believing it was Scriptural only to discover that the Word of God tells us that God helps those who know they *cannot* help themselves (2 Corinthians 12:9-11). You may be like me and you may have repeatedly heard an adage in church, but we must understand that that does not necessarily make it Scriptural. Luke tells us that the Bereans were of more noble character because they examined the Scriptures daily to make sure Paul was teaching them truth (Acts 17:11). We need to do the same. It is imperative that we know what God's Word really is and what it truly says. We cannot blindly trust a man or a religious organization.

The law was originally given as living oracles – as the life-giving words of God Himself. It was not given as rules and regulations. I am not again presenting this distinction because I like to repeat myself; I am emphasizing the importance of proper perception. How we view the Word and how we depict the Word to others is paramount. People have used many words to describe God's Word and many of them have been inaccurate. This spurious portrayal has led many to unfounded beliefs. We must see the Word as God sees it; we must be in agreement with His original intention.

Jeremiah 7:21-24 KJV Thus saith the LORD of hosts…For I spake not unto your fathers, nor commanded them in the day that I brought them out of the land of Egypt, concerning burnt offerings or sacrifices: But this thing commanded I them, saying, Obey My voice, and I will be your God, and ye shall be My people: and walk ye in all the ways that I have commanded you, that it may be well unto you. But they hearkened not, nor inclined their ear, but walked in the counsels [and] in the imagination of their evil heart, and went backward, and not forward.

God's plan was for man to see His Word as their source of Spiritual life. They were not to see it as rules and regulations. What did God really say to man? He told man one thing; He told them to obey His voice. The word translated as obey is again the Hebrew word *shama*. God told them to depend on His Word, but man wanted more. Man added to God's instruction because man wanted to perform and achieve. Man erroneously looked at burnt offerings and sacrifices as something they could do for God, but the burnt offerings and sacrifices had the same purpose as the law – to point man to Christ. Man's desire to perform led to the perversion of the burnt offerings in the same way it led to a perversion or misuse of the Word of God.

> Jeremiah 23:36 NIV But you must not mention 'the oracle of the LORD' again, because every man's own word becomes his oracle and so you distort the words of the living God, the LORD Almighty, our God.

God tells them not to call *their* law *His* oracles. The Word of God has been distorted or perverted by man and we must agree to do so no more. To pervert has been defined as leading someone away from good. I find this interesting because God tells us that He wants to reveal His Son in us so that we may preach Him (Galatians 1:16). The Greek word that was translated as preach means to announce good news. When we turn the Word into anything but good news, we are perverting it - we are leading people away from good. Jesus Christ is good news - living by works is not! We cannot invent our own directive for what God is saying and teach it as truth. God does not concur with man's misdirection. We take the Lord's name in vain when we claim our ideas as His.

God gave living oracles; His plan was good, but because of man's choice to perform, the living words of God became nothing but rules and regulations to those making that choice. What was intended to bring life brought death to those who focused on self rather than Christ. Man looked at the promises of God as challenges and began to use them as a basis to prove what they believed was man's worth and value to God. They lived a selfish life and they produced carnal fruit. This was not God's good plan for us. All along He wanted us to reach out to Him and live through Him. Even though there is no possible way to produce Spiritual fruit on our own many still don't realize their need for a Savior. This may seem confusing at first, but it *must* be understood. That is why it bears repeating. We must see what God sees when we look at the Word. We cannot view the Word as rules (thus putting the focus on self); we must see the Word as Christ, as our Spiritual Seed, if we want to enjoy our new nature in Christ and produce Spiritual fruit.

*　　*　　*

It is important that we study the words that are used in the translation of God's Word. We must be sure of the meaning of the words that we are using. Many times we proclaim boldly what we believe to be true; however, it is not the truth. When we look at the Word of God from our limited perspective we miss the true meaning.

> 1 Timothy 1:7 AMP They are ambitious to be doctors of the Law (teachers of the Mosaic ritual), but they have no understanding either of the words and terms they use or of the subjects about which they make [such] dogmatic assertions.

We may rigidly believe something that is false because we do not understand the original meaning of a word. For example, the King James Version of Luke 14:26 leads some to dogmatically teach that we must not love our parents. A study of the word translated as "hate" reveals the true meaning behind the words of Christ – it means to love less. Scripture will never contradict itself. God tells us to love repeatedly. He even tells us to love those who hate us. When we see a verse that *appears* to contradict another, that is when we need to study more in depth. That is when we need to be sure that what we are so rigidly instructing is actually what God was articulating. There are too many "teachers" misrepresenting the Word.

> Malachi 2:7-8 NIV "For the lips of a priest ought to preserve knowledge, because he is the messenger of the LORD Almighty and people seek instruction from his mouth. But you have turned from the way and by your teaching have caused many to stumble; you have violated the covenant with Levi," says the LORD Almighty.

Those who teach the Word should teach it correctly, but that is not always the case. The Word is not a collection of rules that only the most pious can follow but some teach exactly that. In truth, when we see the Word that way it is defaming God's love and mercy. To believe that we must live up to arduous commands rather than receive God's gift of life is offensive to God's character. Those who teach this are turning from God's loving, life-giving plan and they are leading others down a path of futility.

To view God's Word as His "law" makes some believe that God is not concerned with having a personal relationship with man. The word itself makes us think of rules and regulations, of crime and punishment. It brings many to the wrong conclusion; they conclude that God is only concerned with our performance and that He desires to judge us based on our works and behavior. This also leads to the erroneous belief that only "good" people will go to Heaven and only "good" people will be blessed.

Instead of viewing the Word in this negative light, we must see it as God does. It is our Spiritual Source for Spiritual life. It is everything we need to see Spiritual fruit manifested in our every-day lives. Love, joy, peace, longsuffering, gentleness, goodness, faith, meekness, self-control and temperance, are all the result of abiding in the Word of God. The Word is the Seed we require for every Spiritual fruit. The Word is God's loving provision for His children.

The law was not a mistake that God made when trying to show man how to live. The law was not given as a challenge in order to improve man's behavior. We must view the words of God as they were intended to be perceived. If we do not, we will fall away from God – we will not draw close to Him.

Jeremiah 8:8-9 NIV How can you say, "We are wise, for we have the law of the LORD," when actually the lying pen of the scribes has handled it falsely? The wise will be put to shame; they will be dismayed and trapped. Since they have rejected the Word of the LORD, what kind of wisdom do they have?

The law, the Word of God, was handled falsely. Man handled the Word as a rulebook. Man rejected God's plan for the Word and established their own (Romans 10:3). Man's wisdom, man's theories regarding God's plan, will never produce true wisdom. The wisdom of the world is foolishness to God. Without the Word, we truly do not possess Godly wisdom.

We cannot become wise without the true source of wisdom. The Word tells us that Jesus has become wisdom for us (1 Corinthians 1:30) – He has accomplished what we could not and He is freely sharing it with us. We cannot experience wisdom in our flesh. Our flesh will never be able to produce God's wisdom in the same way a wild donkey would never be able to produce a man as its offspring (Job 11:12).

God often refers to those who deal with the law as those who do not know Him (Jeremiah 2:8). **Man's knowledge of what the Word says does not indicate a relationship with God.** There are some who can quote the Word religiously but they do not understand the truth of the Word. They are focused on self and see the Word as rules and regulations and to be intimate with the law (rules and regulations) is to be estranged from God.

Galatians 5:4 NIV You who are trying to be justified by law have been alienated from Christ; you have fallen away from grace.

We must understand that *our* efforts actually alienate us from God. When we look to be justified by our works we are ignoring what Jesus Christ has done for us and His sacrifice then has no affect on our lives. We reject the grace of God by receiving the malevolent invitation of self-effort. This prideful decision keeps us at a distance from our loving God and it impedes resting in Christ.

Many claim that grace is an excuse to live in sin, but those who do so do not understand the true meaning of grace. The Greek word translated as grace gives us the answer to this false claim. This Greek word's definition shows us that grace is the Divine influence on your heart in your daily life; in other words, it is synonymous with the Word of God or living by faith. Grace is the Word; grace is Jesus Christ. When we live by grace we are living in the Word; Christ is first and we are producing Spiritual fruit because we are being influenced by Him rather than our flesh. It is then impossible for us to sin when we are being influenced by Christ. Grace is not a license to sin; it is our freedom from sin!

When we see the Word as a rulebook, we are living outside of true wisdom and we are falling from grace. We are distancing ourselves from His Divine influence. We are walking in the flesh and the end result will always be the same.

Isaiah 28:9-13 NIV Who is it He is trying to teach? To whom is He explaining His message? To children weaned from their milk, to those just taken from the breast? For it is: Do and do, do and do, rule on rule, rule on rule; a little here, a little there. Very well then, with foreign lips and strange tongues God will speak to this people, to whom He said, "This is the resting place, let the weary rest"; and, "This is the place of repose"-- but they would not listen. So then, the word of the LORD to them will become: Do and do, do and do, rule on rule, rule on rule; a little here, a little there-- so that they will go and fall backward, be injured and snared and captured.

The Word is to be our resting place. We are to *shama* and *shamar* the Word and then experience Christ working though us. The Word is our place of repose, but some ignore this invitation and choose to see it as a challenge. When the Word is viewed as rules and regulations the result will always be backsliding. We can only expect to sink further into the depravity of our flesh when we see the Word this way because flesh can only give birth to flesh. We are not under the influence of the Spirit when we choose to see the Word as rules and rely on self-effort.

The above verses in Isaiah give us a detailed account of viewing the Word of God improperly. It first points out that those who are immature view the Word as a rulebook. It is *not* Spiritual maturity that prompts us to live by self-effort. We see that the immature look at the Word as one rule after another, one work after another. Spiritual maturity is displayed in our dependence on God rather than self.

When God spoke of His Word, He said that it was the resting place for the weary. Jesus also referred to this when He told the weary to come to Him for rest (Matthew 11:28). The Word is our resting place and He is the Word! It is where we go to receive what we need. For example, when we are experiencing a lack of peace in our lives we can go to the Word and find verses on peace. We can then focus on those verses, think about those verses, quote those verses, and so on, instead of trying to be at peace on our own or doing what we deem necessary to earn peace. Our attempt to achieve what can only be received from Christ is wearisome. If you realize that you are weary then you can choose to rest. Do not let pride inhibit rest. The arrogant are never at rest (Habakkuk 2:5 NLT) but you can humble yourself and you can choose to focus on Christ rather than self or situations. As you rest in His promises for peace you will eventually experience peace even in the midst of your circumstances (Philippians 4:7). **Again, the Word of God is the Seed for every Spiritual fruit. Again, we cannot manifest Spiritual fruit in our lives apart from the Word!**

Jesus also told us that His yoke was easy. The root word for the word translated as "easy" means to furnish with what is needed. His Word furnishes us with everything we need for life and for godliness (2 Peter 1:3). We need to look no further. If you remember, one of the definitions for *shama* was to be content – we can be content with the Word alone because nothing else is required. We do not need the word of man when we have the Word of God. We do not need physical proof when we have the promise of God. The Word alone is our necessity.

When we refuse to be content with the Word and refuse to see it as our resting place, then we will view the Word in a perverted manner. This leads us away from God's good plan for us and it turns our perception of the Word into nothing but rules and regulations. When the love letter of the Word becomes rules and regulations to us we will fall backward because we cannot live accordingly. Man can never live by the law. In the book of James, chapter two and verse ten, we are even told that we could keep all of the law except for one part and still be guilty of breaking all of it. That is harsh – *if* you live by the law, but God is not expecting us to live by the law. His plan is for us to live dependent on His Word. When we live dependent on the Word of God then we are free from the demands of the law. We live by grace and not by works. We rest in what Christ has done for us and we participate in our loving Father's good plan.

As we live by grace we find that what is impossible for man is possible for God. For example, it may be impossible for man to tame his tongue, but with God we can speak controllably (James 3:8; Matthew 19:26). We can see Spiritual fruit in our lives through Him alone.

Our perception of the Word is crucial. We must look at the Word as the life-giving Source that God intended for it to be. Whether we call the Bible the Word or the Law makes no difference. It is not about how we label it; what determines our relationship with the Word is how we perceive it. If we view the law as a schoolmaster to lead us to Christ, then the law is grace.   If we erroneously view it as rules and regulations that we believe can keep us in right standing with God, then the law is the opposite of grace - it is the power of sin (1 Corinthians 15:56).

Are we going to see the Word as God intended or as man decided it should be viewed? The choice is ours.

Chapter 5

CHOOSE LIFE OR DEATH

Deuteronomy 30:19 NIV
This day I call heaven and earth as witnesses
against you that I have set before you life and death,
blessings and curses. Now choose life, so that
you and your children may live.

God has always given man freedom of choice. God has never forced His will on anyone. He has clearly presented us with two ways to live – we can choose life or we can choose death. What does this mean? What is life and what is death?

We have already discovered that the Word of God is life (Deuteronomy 32:47). Our choice of life, therefore, *must* include the Word of God. When we choose life we are choosing to live life through Christ by abiding in His Word; in other words, we are living by grace through faith or living life in the Spirit. We are following God's plan to *shama* and *shamar*.

The Bible tells us to live in the same way we received Christ (Colossians 2:6). We received Christ by grace through faith (Ephesians 2:8). We received His free gift; we did nothing to earn it or deserve it. The same will be true in our daily lives. We cannot earn or deserve God's goodness, His kindness, His blessings, His fruit, and so on. We must *receive* everything we need from Him through His Word.

Our understanding of our need to receive from Christ will keep us in the Word of God and that is why we need to be reminded of this need. We need to consistently take in the Word of God. Through our consistent intake of the Word, our hearts will be Divinely influenced and it will become apparent in our daily lives (grace). This choice to focus on Christ rather than self will impart Spiritual life to us and it will bless our children as well. The Word of God will bring life and blessings into our families if we will simply abide in it.

The Word of God is perfect - it is complete; it is everything we need and it will transform our lives. We are told that the Word will convert the soul (Psalms 19:7 KJV). The Word of God will restore us and revive us. The Word brings us back to God's original intention for His creation. The Word will transform our thoughts and our actions. It will revolutionize our feelings and emotions. The Word will make us wise; it will enable us to operate in the nature of Jesus Christ. The Word will keep us from vain attempts to modify our behavior because it will truly transform us. The Bible tells us that when we cleave to the Lord or join ourselves to Him, we are of one Spirit (1 Corinthians 6:17). We can in fact do what Jesus would do when our hearts are being Divinely influenced by His Word because we are of one Spirit; we are like-minded.

God is offering us the gift of Spiritual life but we must receive it daily. To choose life is not simply a one-time decision; it is a lifestyle and we must remind ourselves of this need to choose life. To choose life is to receive the Word and receiving the Word is an ongoing process.

This choice may seem obvious, but to many it has become unclear. The teachings of man have clouded our vision. We have been taught from a young age to achieve. We are taught that if we want something valuable we must work hard for it. This philosophy has penetrated the church and many have fallen for the deception. Man has created their own system, religion, and it has pushed man away from God. The focus has shifted from God to man – man has become dependent on self rather than his Creator. Man has foolishly put his trust in his own works.

Religion has taught us that we need to earn from God rather than receive from Him. It has taught us that God is angry and vengeful, not loving and forgiving. Religion has exchanged the truth for a lie because fear, guilt, and manipulation are powerful tools (Romans 1:25). With tools such as these man can be controlled to a certain degree. Religion has exchanged the truth for a lie by putting the focus on man rather than on God. Religion promotes being self-absorbed rather than God-filled and it does so in a misleading manner. Religion promotes self-effort and pride under the guise of good works and responsibility; however, we must understand that when we fall in line with religion we are choosing death rather than life.

Man has wandered from God's original intention. Man has followed man's ideas rather than God's and in doing so, man has rejected Spiritual life. Man's system can never impart life in the Spirit.

John 6:63 NIV The Spirit gives life; the flesh counts for nothing. The words I have spoken to you are spirit and they are life.

Life is found in Jesus Christ alone and He is the Word. He is the only way to life in the Spirit. Through His Word we can participate in our new, Spiritual nature.

Jesus Himself told us that the flesh counts for nothing, so why then do we choose death? Why do we choose the very thing that is futile? We are stubborn to say the least! Many times I have to try things my way (repeatedly) before I throw my hands up and rest in Christ and receive from Him. I hate doing this, but it is a real struggle because my flesh is a pest. The Bible tells us that the Spirit and the flesh are at war with each other and it means just that. Even though we struggle and we lose battles, we must continue on knowing that ultimately the victory is ours in Christ. We may choose death today, but today isn't over and we have the opportunity to change our mind and choose life now! We can choose life and choose the victory that is ours in Christ without further delay!

Many times we choose death because we are unsure of the truth. Satan is a liar and he has been from the beginning (John 8:44). Satan lied to Eve and she was deceived in the garden (Genesis 3:5). Satan told Eve that she would be like God, but Eve was already made in God's image (Genesis 1:26-27). She must not have been standing firm in that truth because Satan was able to convince her that she had to take matters into her own hands. He made Eve believe that she had to work for something that God had already freely given to her. It's the same today, isn't it? We fall for the lie that says we have to work for God's approval, His love, His blessings, and so on, when Christ already freely gives us every good and perfect gift. As we root ourselves in His truth, Satan's lies will lose their power to persuade.

Satan is a crafty liar; he knows that every prolific lie has a shred of truth. He told Eve that she would know good and evil and that was true, but he didn't tell her that God was protecting her by keeping her from the knowledge of evil. How many times do we fall for the lie that says God is keeping something good from us? I know I have, only to find out that God's plan for me is far better than my own. We can outsmart the devil. We do not have to fall for his lies when we are standing firm in the truth of the Word.

We have to choose - life or death, truth or lies, Spirit or flesh. We cannot live by man's system and God's system simultaneously. We must make a choice.

To choose life is to choose to depend on God rather than on self. It is to look to Him for all that you need. To choose life means to make Christ your priority, your focus. This choice requires humility and reverence for God. We must realize who He is and who we are with Him and who we are apart from Him. To choose life is to cease from works; it is discontinuing our attempts to perform for God and simply learning how to receive from Him through His Word.

Romans 7:4,6 NIV So, my brothers, you also died to the law through the body of Christ, that you might belong to another, to Him who was raised from the dead, in order that we might bear fruit to God…But now, by dying to what once bound us, we have been released from the law so that we serve in the new way of the Spirit, and not in the old way of the written code.

We must die to the law - we must cease all attempts to perform or accomplish because this keeps us in bondage. Jesus Christ is our way out of this bondage. By receiving what He did for us, we are also giving up our own efforts. We cannot choose both. If we want to bear Spiritual fruit, then we must choose life - we must die to the law and find life in Christ alone (Romans 6:11). We cannot try to perform and receive at the same time. Gifts cannot be earned. We are either receiving from Him or we are trying to achieve on our own. We either focus on Him or we focus on self.

Living a life that truly demonstrates the Word of God is never the result of man's effort; it is the result of filling ourselves with the Word of God to the point that it is overflowing into our daily lives. When we choose the Seed of the Word, Spiritual fruit will be produced. What seed we plant is imperative. Choose the Seed of the Word today and anticipate your harvest of Spiritual fruit.

Chapter 6

TRUTH OR CONSEQUENCES

Galatians 3:10 NIV
All who rely on observing the law are under a curse, for it is written: "Cursed is everyone who does not continue to do everything written in the Book of the Law."

As I read the above verse I wonder why I ever thought that living by works was God's plan, but the enemy is crafty and many are deceived and choose works over grace just like I did for so many fruitless years. The enemy will take the Word of God and twist verses. He will lead us to believe that certain verses apply to us when they in fact do not. He will lead us to see the Word as rules and regulations rather than a covenant of loving promises. He works hard to lead us away from the truth of grace because he knows the consequences of the law. Even though his efforts seem relentless, we can know that our God of truth is greater and we can live blessed rather than cursed! The enemy's plan to deceive can be thwarted if we focus on Christ rather than self. Our choice to focus on Christ rather than self will set us free from the lies of the enemy because abiding in the Word of truth produces freedom (John 8:31-32). No longer will we live under the curse of works or self-effort when Christ is our focus.

The *curse* of works or self-effort - do we see our attempts to live up to the law as a *curse*? We should! God defines our works as filthy rags in His sight and we should do the same (Isaiah 64:6). Our self-effort is a curse because we are choosing self over God. What would make us believe that we could ever live up to God's standards on our own? It is pride.   If we choose to live by works, then we have to understand what that truly means.

Galatians 4:21 NIV Tell me, you who want to be under the law, are you not aware of what the law says?

The truth of the Word teaches us that we cannot live by works because we have no righteousness of our own outside of Christ.   This truth teaches us that living by the law is therefore futile. Are we aware of this? We see this futility in the book of James when we are told that if you break one part of the law you are guilty of breaking it all (James 2:10). Who then could ever truly live up to the law and live by works? No one. We need to be aware of the truth. None of us could bear the punishments of the law - no one truly did, as a matter of fact. The consequences of the law would have killed off every human being that ever existed. Are we aware of that?

The Word also tells us that those who live by the law will actually be controlled by sin because the power of sin is the law (1 Corinthians 15:56). No wonder we are under a curse when we choose to live by the law. The choice of self-effort is a forfeiture of receiving from Christ and that will never lead us to life in the Spirit; it leads to a cursed life, a life of living in sin, a life controlled by the flesh.

2 Peter 2:19 NLT …For you are a slave to whatever controls you.

Are you controlled by self? Are you controlled by guilt, fear, condemnation, comparison, pride, envy, and so on, or are you controlled by Christ? When we choose to live by works we are not controlled by Christ. We are driven by the list above and more! Living by works makes man the source and that makes sin the result because anything that is not of faith is sin (Romans 14:23). Faith comes from our consistent intake of the Word and faith produces Spiritual fruit in our lives (Romans 10:17). When we are ignoring the Word in our lives, then Spiritual fruit is elusive and sin prevails. Any fruit that does not come from the Seed of the Word is sin. The only way we can escape the power of sin is through Christ / the Word.

> Romans 6:14 NIV For sin shall no longer be your master, because you are not under the law, but under grace.

When we live under the law then sin is our master. Living under the law (or by works) gives sin power over us. We are being controlled by a carnal source when we are living by works and seeing God's Word as nothing but rules and regulations. When we live by grace (by receiving the Word to the point that it is our main influence) sin will no longer control us. The Word of God keeps us from sin. The power of sin is defeated in the presence of Christ. Sin can no longer control the person who is under Divine influence.

Who is controlling you? Is Christ controlling you? If Christ is in control then the fruit in your life will reveal His presence. When I am grouchy, irritable and easily offended, I am revealing who is in control in my life - my flesh.

Jesus went to the home of Mary and Martha and spoke to them about the consequences of choosing works over grace (Luke 10:38-42). Mary sat at the feet of Jesus and she received from Him. She was taking in His Word and being

Divinely influenced; she was living by grace through faith. Martha was busy. She was working. She was trying to do something for Jesus rather than receive from Him; as a result, she was placing blame on Mary and complaining. Jesus told Martha that she was anxious and troubled about many things but only one thing was necessary. She did not understand that receiving from Christ was the one thing - the one thing that is eternal, the only thing that really matters. Receiving from Christ is the one thing that will take care of every other thing. It is the one thing that makes our works Spiritual rather than carnal. Martha would still need to prepare the meal, but now she could do it through Christ rather than through her own self-efforts by simply receiving from Him first.

How many times do we go it alone? I know I lived many years anxious and troubled about many things because I was not receiving what I needed from Christ. I was my own idol.

Isaiah 44:20 NLT The poor, deluded fool feeds on ashes. He trusts something that can't help him at all. Yet he cannot bring himself to ask, "Is this idol that I'm holding in my hand a lie?"

I thought I had to perform and be good enough. I was

a poor, deluded fool. I was believing the lie of works without even questioning its validity. I was trusting blindly in self while ignoring the fact that I cannot help myself at all! For too long I did not realize that Christ made me good and He would work through me if I only gave Him the opportunity. I praise God for His eye-opening truth! I now know that living by works is a lie. I now know that Christ alone enables me to see transformation. Just like Martha, the appearance of the things I do has not changed much - she still would have made the meal after she received from Christ in the same way I still go to church, I still read the Word, and so on; however, now the Source of those actions is Christ and no longer self. He is my priority and He is my Source. He leads me into the things of the Spirit. I am receiving from Christ and He is working through me and now the things I do are of eternal value rather than filthy rags.

> 1 Corinthians 3:13 KJV Every man's work shall be made manifest: for the day shall declare it, because it shall be revealed by fire; and the fire shall try every man's work of what sort it is.

What sort of work is being produced in your life? Is it Spiritual or carnal? Although we cannot always see the source of our actions today, one day it will be apparent. Paul goes on to say that works of the flesh will be destroyed; they will not last. Jesus told Martha that what Mary did could not be taken from her because she was receiving from Him. What is done through Christ will last; it is eternal. What we do on our own will be burned up; it is temporary. When we choose to live by works or our own self-effort we are choosing the fleeting pleasure of sin. We may feel good about ourselves for a while, others may praise us, and so on, but our efforts will never be able to produce eternal blessings.

Our carnal efforts may not be noticed by others as carnal but the fruit those efforts produce sure will be. Martha was complaining and she was placing blame on Mary because of her source; she was producing the opposite of the fruit of the Spirit and it was noticeable. When our source is Christ we will be at peace and we will not feel the need to criticize, blame and complain. Our hearts will be full of love that we cannot help but give out to others. Christ in me will display His goodness and love, but when I am full of self that we will be apparent as well.

Living in the temporary is a cursed life. We must understand the choice we are making when we choose to ignore the Word of God in our daily lives. The Word of God is the only Seed for Spiritual fruit. We cannot see a Spiritual harvest without it. Whether we agree or not, whether we like to read or not, we must realize this truth. For those of you who hate to read, I suggest you start small. Take in a few verses a day. As you continue on in the Word you will notice that your desire for the Word will increase. The Word will produce the Spiritual fruit of Spiritual desire in you. Your Spiritual appetite will increase and soon a few verses will not be enough. You will find yourself reading for hours and won't even realize it. When we try to make ourselves read it will be an arduous task. We will be bored and we will not receive what Christ truly longs to give. Stop trying to live the Christian life apart from Christ. He is the Source. We cannot do it without Him! He is your loving Savior and His arms are open wide ready to embrace you and provide you with every good thing you need.

Truth or consequences. Reject His love or embrace it. Draw close to Him or cling to your flesh. Live in the Word or live controlled by the flesh. The choice is yours and the choice is mine and we must be aware of the significance of our choice.

Chapter 7

Crime and Punishment

Isaiah 1:5 AMP

Why should you be stricken and punished
any more [since it brings no correction]?
You will revolt more and more. The whole
head is sick, and the whole heart is faint
(feeble, sick, and nauseated).

The rebellion of man is not due to an absence of consequences – its cause is a Spiritual disease; therefore, punishment cannot rectify rebellion. The whole head is sick – the mind of man is diseased without the Word of God (Romans 8:7). The whole head is sick - the mind controlled by the flesh is weak and unhealthy; it is full of sin. The mind controlled by the flesh will never produce Spiritual fruit. We must renew our minds with the Word if we want to live as God intended (Romans 12:2). If we choose to view the Word as irrelevant and not worth our time, then we will be controlled by our flesh (Romans 1:28). God describes the mind of the flesh as worthless and depraved; He says that the mind of the flesh leads us to do exactly what we shouldn't do. When a mind is controlled by the flesh even man's misplaced desire for punishment will prove futile.

Our hearts are faint – man is weak, troubled and overwhelmed by life apart from God. We cannot live a strong victorious life apart from Jesus Christ. The absence of the Word in man's life is the cause of all evil.

God never claimed punishment as His plan. God told man the answer for their depravity: *shama* and *shamar* His Word. Are we in agreement with God's plan? Do we see the Word as our Spiritual life? The Word is the prescription for the flesh and all that it produces. The Word of God is Spiritual health and healing for all who receive it. Time and time again, however, man chooses to live by performance or works, and works have consequences. Man chooses self over God repeatedly and mankind has suffered as a result.

Living by works includes punishment and reward. Each law had its own punishment if it were to be broken and reward if kept. Man's carnal nature embraced this system. Man arrogantly believed they were good enough and they could conquer the system; however, they were proven wrong. Even still, some persist in believing they are good enough to earn from God. Some feel that their behavior should earn them a free trip to heaven and blessings here on earth. Then there are those who know they cannot be good enough so they give up and decide to ignore God because they have the wrong perception of God. Either way, living by works never draws us close to God.

Crime and punishment put the focus on man. Can man perform? Can man achieve? Punishment was presented and executed, but it could never bring about transformation. Punishment may cause some to modify their behavior, but it can never truly transform the heart and mind of man - only the Word of God / Jesus Christ can.

Let's examine the law of an eye for an eye, for example. When we first see the act of murder addressed in the Old Testament we witness God providing protection in the midst of the consequences when Cain cried out to God (Genesis 4:9-15). Murder was not the right thing for Cain to do - murder is sin - but God protected Cain's life. Cain took the life of his brother and he had to deal with the consequences; nonetheless, God still showed him mercy. God did not take his life; that was not God's plan. An eye for eye became the standard as man attempted to accomplish the law on his own, but even the punishment could not keep man from the act of murder. The fear of retribution and retribution itself cannot transform man; it can never keep man from sin.

Man continues to look at the punishment and view it as something that can prevent sin, but that is not the case. The law and its punishments were harsh yet sin could not be contained. The law was designed by God to point us to our need for Christ, but man does not always recognize their need and they refuse to cry out for help like Cain did. Peter is an example of this refusal to cry out to God for help because of a flawed sense of trust in self-effort (Matthew 6:33-35, 69-75). Jesus told Peter he would deny Him, but Peter refused to believe it. (Christ told us that apart from Him we could do nothing of Spiritual value, also. Do we believe it?) Peter ignored the words of Christ and boldly declared *his* love and *his* devotion only to find himself doing the very thing he vehemently promised *he* would not do. We need Christ. We cannot avoid the flesh without Him.

As man continues in his decadent state of pride, sin abounds. The law of an eye for an eye should have led man to Christ; it should have opened their eyes to their desperate need for a Savior, but pride got in the way. Instead of calling on God for the help they required, they persisted in their dead way of living by works.

As man continued to view the Word as the law (a list of rules and regulations) rather than living oracles, man's perception of God became distorted as well. How we view our Savior and His love letter to us is paramount. We cannot be reminded of this enough.

> Job 10:13-14 NIV But this is what You concealed in Your heart, and I know that this was in Your mind: If I sinned, You would be watching me and would not let my offense go unpunished.

For a time, Job looked at God the wrong way. He saw God as vengeful and ready to pounce. He viewed Him as one who readily convicts and punishes harshly. Job thought that God was in heaven just waiting for him to make a mistake. How many people see Him the same way today? Religion has facilitated this perception and has managed to make it deceptively attractive. Phrases, such as, "God is watching you," have become foreboding rather than comforting (as God intended). Some egotistical people revel in this sinister misrepresentation. They love to see God portrayed as angry and vengeful and I can only believe it's because they think they are good enough to avoid punishment and they look forward to seeing others punished because they believe they certainly have it coming to them. They do not take the focus off of themselves and others long enough to consider the Father's love as the reason He is watching. God is watching over us because He loves us, but living by works has led man to believe that God is watching to make sure He sees you fall so that He can punish you when you deserve it. What an awful way to see our loving Redeemer!

As we look through God's Word we will see examples of His mercy throughout. How many times did man break the law and God showed them mercy? Too many to count, I am sure! If man truly lived by the law, mankind would be extinct! Nehemiah points this out as He declares God's goodness, mercy, and His readiness to forgive (Nehemiah 9:16-21, 31); unfortunately, some people are not impacted by His mercy. Those who live in the flesh disregard His goodness.

Isaiah 26:10 NIV But when grace is shown to the wicked, they do not learn righteousness; even in a land of uprightness they go on doing evil and do not regard the majesty of the LORD.

Every single person that has ever existed has been shown the grace, mercy and favor of God. For some, they ignore it and reject it and they are consequently unaffected by it. For others, they accept it and embrace it and it transforms them. I want to accept it and embrace it consistently and I am sure you do too! I want to live affected by His love.

Jesus Christ loves us so much. He has paid the price for our punishment because of this love and when we truly understand this, we will never fear punishment again.

Romans 4:8 NIV Blessed is the man whose sin the Lord will never count against him.

What a blessing it is to know that our sins are paid for because of what Jesus Christ has done for us. Sin can eat away at you and destroy you if you do not understand this. Fear and guilt will torture you when you do not realize what Christ has done for you because He loves you. Our understanding of His perfect love, however, will dispel fear (1 John 4:18). In the book of Genesis (chapters 37 through 50) we read about a young man named Joseph. Joseph was mistreated by his brothers - and not mistreated as some define mistreatment. His brothers despised him to the point that they wanted to kill him, but instead found opportunity to sell him as a slave. As God's plan for Joseph unfolds we find that in the course of time Joseph becomes a great leader and his brothers end up needing his help. The same brothers who sold him as a slave (and covered their sin by telling their father that Joseph died), now need his help. When they realized that Joseph was the one that could help them, they were filled with fear. Fear that was the result of the guilt of their sin. In their hearts they had been fearing punishment and now they were faced with that very possibility. They did not understand forgiveness. Even after Joseph told them that he forgave them, they still believed the other shoe would drop at any time. Guilt is a load that man was never meant to bear; in fact, we *cannot* bear it.

>Psalms 38:4 NIV My guilt has overwhelmed me like a burden too heavy to bear.

Guilt is overwhelming and it will overpower us if we allow it access into our lives. Guilt is too much for man to bear. As a result of man's effort to attempt to deal with guilt, some guilt-laden people commit suicide, some turn to addiction, some lean on hate and become judgmental, some become obsessive and on and on the list goes. Only Jesus Christ can free us from the guilt that sin produces (Psalm 32:5). We can find freedom from sin *and* guilt when we turn to Him. He paid the price for us - the entire price. There is nothing left for us to pay. There are those that will say that this way of thinking leads some to believe that God is "soft" on sin. If we would simply look at exactly what Jesus Christ had to go through because of our sin, we would understand how erroneous that way of thinking is. God is not soft on sin, but He is just. Jesus Christ took the punishment for our sin and our guilt and God accepted it as payment in full - He will never require anything else from us. We have been made right with God through Jesus Christ. God sees us through Christ.

> 2 Corinthians 5:18-19 NIV All this is from God, who reconciled us to Himself through Christ and gave us the ministry of reconciliation: that God was reconciling the world to Himself in Christ, not counting men's sins against them. And He has committed to us the message of reconciliation.

We have been reconciled. What does that mean? It means that Christ has made us right with God. He put an end to the separation between God and man that sin created. He made us acceptable and highly favored. We are now one with Christ and God loves us like He loves Christ

> John 17:22-23 NIV I have given them the glory that You gave Me, that they may be one as we are one— I in them and You in Me—so that they may be brought to complete unity. Then the world will know that You sent Me and have loved them even as You have loved

Me.

Jesus Christ paid the price for me so that I could receive His glory and be one with Him. That is awe-inspiring. As I read these verses I am left speechless. I am overwhelmed by the love He has for me. I need to remind myself of this love daily and I need to share this with others. He has committed to us this message of reconciliation. We are to spread the good news! We have been made right with God because of Jesus Christ! Instead, too many people are taking the name of God in vain and declaring another message and they are leading people away from the good news of reconciliation. They are trying to scare people into submission by portraying God as vengeful and eager to punish. People are portraying God as an unforgiving God instead of the God of love that He is and they are doing this as though they were His messengers. There are some who hate "Christians" but they do not realize that they are hating people who are *not* Christ-like in the least. The message of Christ is not one of condemnation or criticism.

Jesus Christ took our punishment and gave us His righteousness. He is not counting our sins against us; He wants to save us from our sins (John 3:17). Wow! That leaves me in awe of my awesome, loving, forgiving Father and that is *exactly* what it is supposed to do.

We have been made right with God through Christ. Will we humble ourselves and learn to be receivers or will we continue to try to earn what has already been freely given?

Chapter 8

HUMILITY OR PRIDE

Proverbs 3:34 NIV

He mocks proud mockers but

gives grace to the humble.

God gives grace to the humble. Grace, or the Divine influence on the heart and its reflection in your daily life, is for those who are humble. The humble realize their need for the Word and they are not too proud to receive it. Grace is a gift – it cannot be earned or deserved. In order for us to be influenced by God daily we must receive from Him and receiving requires humility. The humble go to the Word regularly to *receive* everything that they require – they know that they cannot do anything Spiritual on their own so they are not trying to earn or deserve anything from God (John 15:5).

The proud, on the other hand, are "mocked" by God. When we look at the definition of mock we see that it has several meanings, but one stands out: to prevent something.

We are prevented from producing Spiritual fruit in our flesh. Only Spirit can give birth to something Spiritual (John 3:6). When our carnal attempts fail we find ourselves frustrated and at times humiliated – if this leads us to Christ, then it has done its job; however, it does not always do so. Some walk away from the frustration of the flesh and try harder and some walk away feeling humiliated and abandon what they thought was their relationship with God. That happened to me.

I viewed the Word as rule upon rule and I was *not* enjoying a personal relationship with God – I was living nothing more than a religious lie. Religion is man-made rules and ideas; whereas, Christianity is a personal relationship with Jesus Christ. Religion is man's idea of how to impress or please God; it is not based on what Christ has done for man but what man mistakenly believes that they can do for God. Many have deserted the church because of religion – they attempt to live by the rules only to find that they are lacking and rather than continue on in the losing battle, they simply remove themselves from the fight.

Too many have left what they believe to be the church when in fact they were leaving a religious system that God is not a part of. God is not placing demands on man – man has placed them on man. Man's pride has led to the institution of religion. Pride believes that man can achieve what God has told us is impossible.

As we discussed previously, God gave us His Word, living oracles, and His prescription for man was to live through Him but man had another idea.

Exodus 24:3 NIV When Moses went and told the people all the LORD's words and laws, they responded with one voice, "Everything the LORD has said we will do."

Pride made the Israelites believe that they could perform *for* God. They arrogantly proclaimed *their* ability to carry out the Word but quickly displayed their inability – before long they were making a calf out of gold to worship.

We must understand that any attempt we make at conquering the law will always end in defeat. We are arrogant and deceived if we believe anything contrary. We cannot perform the law or live up to it – we are Spiritually helpless apart from Christ.

John 15:4-5 NIV Remain in Me, and I will remain in you. No branch can bear fruit by itself; it must remain in the vine. Neither can you bear fruit unless you remain in Me. I am the vine; you are the branches. If a man remains in Me and I in him, he will bear much fruit; apart from Me you can do nothing.

We are the branches and no branch can bear fruit by itself. This is humbling. The fruit on the branch would not exist without the vine; it is the result of the vine. We must realize that we rely on Christ – He is not depending on us. We do not support the root, the root supports us (Romans 11:18)! If we desire Spiritual fruit, then we must abide in Christ – He is our Spiritual Source (and continue to remember, He is the Word). We cannot produce Spiritual fruit unless we are remaining in Him by abiding in the Word.

As long as we ignore our desperate need for Christ, we will continue in our flesh. Any solo effort will be for naught; we will never see any Spiritual manifestation because of our carnal efforts.   We must humble ourselves and depend on Him.

Jeremiah 44:10 NIV   To this day they have not humbled themselves or shown reverence, nor have they followed My law and the decrees I set before you and your fathers.

God set *His* law before them – His living oracles, His plan for man to *shama* and *shamar*. We must never forget God's intention. God gave them His Word as living oracles but they ignored His provision and continued to live by the works of their flesh. Their pride hindered their relationship with God and pride continues to get in the way today.

God reveals that they were too stubborn and prideful to follow His Word. The Hebrew word that was translated as "follow" is *halak*. To walk, be eased, go after, and to be weak, are a few of the principal definitions for *halak*. Each describes what our relationship with the Word should be.

We should walk in the Word – we should spend time exploring the Word, going to and fro. A walk is a series of steps; a walk takes time. We must keep stepping if we want to take a walk. The Word of God must be progressively explored; we must humbly continue to discover the love and life of God daily because we need it.

To "follow" the Word is to also be at ease. We should be at ease when we are in the Word – we should not feel pressure because of the Word. The Word is to be our place of rest. The Word is our mirror showing us who we are in Christ; it is not a rulebook we have to try to live up to. Feelings of pressure and stress are the result of looking at the Word the wrong way. Seeing the Word as rules promotes self-absorption – we are focusing on self rather than Christ when we are trying to live by works. *Christ* is our righteousness! We have no hope of being righteous without Him. We cannot produce Spiritual fruit apart from Him! **Stress is a result of trying to do something that is impossible – we cannot produce Spiritual fruit without Him; and if we try, then we will be left with stress-filled feelings of insecurity and pressure.**

Pride is deceptive; while others look at us and believe that we have it all together, we are really living in a prison of doubt and feelings of insignificance. God's desire is for us to humbly walk in His Word and rest in what *He* has done for us. God wants us to look at the Word as promises, not rules. He wants us to look at it as a mirror - He wants us to see who we are in Christ when we are reading. He wants us to be at ease because we know the Word will transform us into all He created us to be if we simply abide in it and receive from Him.

A person who "follows" the Word goes after the Word. They pursue the Word by making it part of their daily life. As we begin to truly understand that the Word is our life and not just a bunch of rules and regulations that we cannot possibly keep up with, we will then pursue the Word in our daily lives. Our pursuit of the Word is the result of our understanding of the purpose of the Word.

When we "follow" we also recognize our weakness. We pursue the Word because we know from where true strength comes. Pride inhibits our pursuit of the Word. We will never depend on the Word if we ignore our weakness and continue to depend on ourselves.

The proud look at the Word as a challenge and take pleasure in their counterfeit ability to perform and attempt to live *for* God. The humble look at the Word as their source of Spiritual life and fruit; and therefore, they live *through* Christ.

Romans 15:17-18 KJV I have therefore whereof I may glory through Jesus Christ in those things which pertain to God. I will not venture to speak of anything except what CHRIST has accomplished through me...

Paul understood his weakness. He would glory – which means to rejoice or boast – through Christ for all of the Spiritual fruit in his life. The phrase, "those things which pertain to God," depicts Spiritual fruit and he understood that Christ alone was the source of that accomplishment. Paul was humble; consequently, Christ was manifested in his life. He would boast about what *Christ* had done. He rejoiced in

His Savior because he was humble and he realized where true Spiritual fruit came from.

> 1 Corinthians 4:7 NIV For who makes you different from anyone else? What do you have that you did not receive? And if you did receive it, why do you boast as though you did not?

Boasting is the result of believing a religious lie. Every good and perfect gift is from above (James 1:17) and we should live thankful rather than prideful.

Do we venture to speak of all that we do for God or do we proclaim the work of Christ in our lives? Do we brag about how much we love God or do we delight in His love for us? Are we giving the glory to God or are we taking pride in ourselves? I know that I lived out the lie of self-effort. I believed it was my self-effort that made me right with God and I was tormented most of the time. I had my days when I felt good about myself but they were few and far between. As I look back now, I see how arrogant it was to believe that I had pleased God. Today I know that any Spiritual fruit I produce is only because of Him and the work He does in me so I live life a lot more thankful than I used to (Acts 3:26). I have my days still; I still struggle at times with believing lies about my identity and my performance. I thank God that I am moving forward and progressively learning to ignore the lies. His Word is alive and at work in me and the lies cannot take root like they used to. It is up to us how we will live - based on lies or truth. We must choose to focus on Christ rather than self and we must do so repeatedly. Your self-centered flesh will rear its ugly head every chance it gets. That is why we cannot let the things that we have been learning slip from our remembrance. Repetition is key. We cannot be reminded enough of this life-transforming truth.

Humble yourself by shifting your focus from self to Christ and begin to live a Spiritually fruitful life that is full of thanksgiving and joy all thanks to Jesus Christ!

Chapter 9

NO MORE CONDEMNATION

Romans 8:1 KJV

There is therefore now no condemnation to them which are in Christ Jesus, who walk not after the flesh, but after the Spirit.

I begin to leave condemnation behind when I realize who I am in Christ (as the result of abiding in the Word). When I walk after the flesh I will be susceptible to condemnation and guilt. Living free of condemnation is not the result of behaving properly; it is the result of an ever-increasing knowledge of who I am in Christ and what He has already taken care of for me. As I continue to learn more about Christ I also begin to walk in the good things He has purchased for me.

Do we really understand what Christ has done for us and who He is to us? For too many years I believed that Christ was mad at me or disappointed in me when I would sin. This misconception kept me from an intimate relationship with my loving Savior and it lead me deeper into a carnal existence. I did not realize the truth, and the lie kept me from receiving the help I needed from Christ to turn things around.

> 1 John 2:1-3 KJV   My little children, these things write I unto you, that ye sin not. And if any man sin, we have an advocate with the Father, Jesus Christ the righteous: And He is the propitiation for our sins: and not for ours only, but also for the sins of the whole world. And hereby we do know that we know Him, if we keep His commandments.

The Word was written for me. God gave His Word to me to keep me from sin. As I hide the Word in my heart it gives me the power and strength I need to reject sin's influence in my life. Unfortunately, I do not always live this out in my daily life. Praise God, however, the verse doesn't end there. God is aware that we are human, that we are simply dust, and that we will never be free from our flesh while we are in these earthly bodies (Psalm 103:11-14). He knows our weaknesses and He has provided us with an advocate for such times.

What is an advocate? An advocate is a someone who supports someone. They back them; they further and promote them. When you are an advocate for someone you intercede for them and you defend them; you justify and vindicate them.

An advocate also comforts and consoles; they favor. As I read and reread the traits of an advocate I am overwhelmed and in awe of the love God has for me. God is not waiting to "get me" when I sin; He is waiting to support me, to comfort me, to vindicate and justify me. Wow! If that doesn't inspire awe and reverence for God then I am not sure what will!

Instead of punishment or retribution, God is advocating for His children through Christ. If I am living under guilt and condemnation it is not by God's choice; it is because I am choosing to ignore the truth of the Word and focus on lies.

He is the propitiation for my sins. He has made atonement for me. He endured my punishment; the punishment I could not bear. He took my place and when I choose to live under guilt and condemnation I am saying that what He did for me was not enough. I am saying that I have to pay part of the price. That is pride to believe I can pay part. That is making self your focus and your idol. That is rejection of truth.

John also tells us that when we "keep His commandments" we will know that we know Him. As I keep (guard, protect, focus on,...) His commandments (His prescription, His Word) I will come to know Him more intimately. I will begin to see Him the right way. I will see

Him as my advocate and my propitiation and I will reject the temptation to live in shame, guilt, blame, and condemnation - and I will reject the temptation to condemn, blame, shame, and guilt others as well. My life will become Christ-centered rather than self-centered. He will increase and I will decrease when I focus on His Word and guard it in my life.

I believe we have options concerning sin. We can choose to ignore sin, we can choose to revel in it, we can choose to condemn ourselves, or we can choose to go to God for the power to overcome sin. Believing the lie that says we should feel guilty and shameful because of sin will keep us from going to God and that is destructive because He is the only One who can give us victory over sin. To so desperately desire and need the love, affection, and support of your heavenly Father while feeling as if you cannot possibly deserve it leads to immense feelings of loneliness, shame, and guilt and it leads us down a path of overwhelming fear, doubt, and anxiety. We heap sin upon sin when we live in condemnation. We begin to dig ourselves in deeper and deeper when we live under guilt and shame. It is *never* Spiritual to feel guilty. The Spiritual answer to sin is not shame and blame; it is freedom through Jesus Christ. My Spiritual nature will give me the ability to see sin for what it is and it will give me the power to overcome it through the Word of God.

> 2 Corinthians 7:10 NIV Godly sorrow brings repentance that leads to salvation and leaves no regret, but worldly sorrow brings death.

When we are led by the Spirit to see sin for what it is, it will lead to a change of mind. We will move away from that sin and on to a closer relationship with the Lord. Worldly sorrow is guilt, condemnation, and the like, and it brings death or simply more of the flesh. Guilt and its cohorts put the focus on you rather than Christ. They are of the flesh and they will never bring about anything Spiritual in your life. We must remember that His *kindness* leads us to repentance or that change of mind that leads to a changed life (Romans 2:4). If we desire Spiritual transformation, then we must realize that Christ is our advocate when we sin. He will renew our minds and lead us deeper into the things of the Spirit if we stay focused on Him rather than self. Our attention to the Word will lead to a Spiritual transformation. We cannot remain the same when we are abiding in the Word. The Word works!

As we focus on Christ, rather than self, we will begin to see ourselves as the dearly loved children that we are. We will see ourselves as more than conquerors and we will realize the power we have in Christ. We will begin to abide in the truth and thereby we will experience the freedom only Christ can give. Instead of living under guilt and condemnation, we will rejoice in what Christ has done for us.

> Colossians 2:13-15 NIV When you were dead in your sins and in the uncircumcision of your flesh, God made you alive with Christ. He forgave us all our sins, having canceled the charge of our legal indebtedness, which stood against us and condemned us; He has taken it away, nailing it to the cross. And having disarmed the powers and authorities, He made a public spectacle of them, triumphing over them by the cross.

Every sin I have ever committed or will commit has been erased - as far as the east is from the west! He canceled out the charges that were against me according to the law. The law was against me, it condemned me, but He took it all and nailed it to the cross! The guilt, the blame, the shame, the accusation - all of it is *gone* thanks to Jesus Christ! And because of what He did for me, the enemy is stripped of his power over me. The flesh has been defeated! He has obtained victory for me and no longer do I have to live as a prisoner to my flesh. I can control my flesh rather than giving it permission to control me. I can receive what Christ did for me and live through Him victorious over my flesh. Praise God!

We need to be in our rightful place, in the Spirit as victorious Christians, if we are going to see Spiritual fruit produced in our lives. We must realize what is rightfully ours in Christ and we must realize all that Christ does for us.

John 15:1-2 KJV I am the true vine, and My Father is the husbandman. Every branch in Me that beareth not fruit He taketh away: and every branch that beareth fruit, He purgeth it, that it may bring forth more fruit.

My misunderstanding of these verses (and others like them) were the cause of many sleepless nights until I began to dig. The words translated as "taketh away" mean to lift up or expiate sin; to bear up or carry. When I am not bearing fruit it is because I am not in my rightful place; therefore, He will lift me up and remind me that my sin has been paid for. When I am wallowing in the dust, like a vine that is on the ground, I cannot bear fruit. I cannot bear fruit because I am not in a Spiritual place. It is not Spiritual to wallow in guilt and condemnation; it is carnal! It is carnal or of the flesh because it disagrees with the Word of God. The Bible tells us that we are forgiven and we are seated in heavenly places with Christ

Jesus because of His great love for us (Ephesians 2:4-6). I need to be in my rightful place - I need to be in His presence - if I want to see Spiritual fruit produced. And when I am bearing fruit, I need to continue to be reminded that I am the righteousness of God in Christ only because of what He has done; it is never because of something I did. We are to seek *His* righteousness (Matthew 6:33), not our own. My focus needs to remain on Christ. I need to look to Him rather than myself. I need to remember that the law, sin and all it entails has been nailed to the cross for me because He loves me so (Colossians 2:14). Christ publicly announced to the devil and every demon force that I am free! I am victorious!

We have so much to be thankful for and so much to celebrate. It reminds me of Hezekiah (2 Chronicles 30:18-27). The people did contrary to what was written in the law and Hezekiah was moved to pray for them. He was moved to call on God and His goodness. The goodness of our loving God overrides the law! When the people experienced His goodness and His forgiveness the result was celebration, joy and praise. Are you living a life of celebration, joy, and praise? You should be! In the next chapter of second Chronicles we also see that they destroyed their false gods. His goodness leads to repentance - a change of mind that transforms our lives (Romans 2:4). Too many Christians are living lifeless. They are depressed and sorrowful because they do not understand the truth concerning what Christ did for them and instead of being captivated by His love, they are held captive by their flesh. Life is not celebrated, it is tolerated. Life is not a royal reign, it is a royal pain. They are producing sin and they are miserable. It is time for us to acknowledge the good Christ has done for us and move on from guilt and condemnation to the good things God has provided.

> Philemon 1:6 NIV I pray that your partnership with us in the faith may be effective in deepening your understanding of every good thing we share for the sake of Christ.

Paul wanted the end result of his partnership with other Christians to be their extensive understanding of every good thing that was theirs because of Christ. He understood the charge of the ministry of reconciliation. He spoke of God's goodness and He spoke of keeping Christ as your focus. Guilt and condemnation are not good things; they are not Spiritual. They are things that keep us as the focus of our own lives rather than Christ and that is never good because it is living in the flesh.

The flesh will lead us into condemnation but the flesh

can also lead us into pride - both of which are equally evil. We must understand the difference between what is Spiritual and what is of the flesh. We must recognize condemnation and pride at their onset. Stay focused on Christ by abiding in the Word and that will keep you from anything that tries to distract you from the goodness of your God.

Chapter 10

THE WORD WORKS

2 Corinthians 12:9 KJV

And He said unto me, My grace is sufficient for thee: for My strength is made perfect in weakness. Most gladly therefore will I rather glory in my infirmities, that the power of Christ may rest upon me.

The word works. It is everything we need to live a Spiritual life. Unfortunately, man has a hard time accepting that. I know I have struggled with accepting it. We want to add to the Word. We want to add our thoughts, our ideas, our dead works, and so on, but Jesus very clearly told us that the Word is all that is required.

Paul was a man just like you and me. He struggled at times also. Paul had a thorn and he went to Christ to talk about it. When Paul asked for freedom from the thorn in his flesh, Jesus simply answered that His grace was sufficient. What exactly does that mean? Was Jesus giving Paul a lackadaisical response or is there a depth to His answer that we do not find when we simply surface read? There is depth! We have found that grace is the Divine influence on the heart in our daily lives. Grace is synonymous with the Word of God. His grace is sufficient so that means the Word is sufficient. The Greek word that sufficient was translated from provides us with the depth of this truth. This Greek word means to raise a barrier and to ward off. It also means to be of value or use to, to be profitable and advantageous. It means to be forceful and effective, worthy and useful. Finally we see that it means to serve, to help, and to be enough. These descriptors show us the depth of Jesus' answer to the thorn of the flesh and they show us that the Word is amazing and it is clearly all that we need to live the victorious, Spiritual life that Christ died for us to live.

> 2 Timothy 3:16-17 NIV   All Scripture is God-breathed and is useful for teaching, rebuking, correcting, and training in righteousness, so that the servant of God may be thoroughly equipped for every good work.

The Word works. It will do what God promised. The Word is useful *in righteousness* - the Word shows us who we are in Christ. It teaches us of our new nature and it corrects us when we begin to fall for the lies of the flesh. We cannot produce Spiritual fruit, or every good work, when we are not participating in our new, righteous nature; consequently, the Word will guide us back to our right standing in Christ.

The Word of God is our advantage over the flesh. It will raise up a barrier and ward off the flesh if we will simply use it. It is effective for righteousness. We saw earlier that we cannot wallow in the dust or in our flesh and still produce Spiritual fruit. The branch that is not producing fruit needs to be lifted up to its proper place. We need to be in our proper place - His righteousness. We are the righteousness of God in Christ and the Word will keep us focused on our Spiritual identity. When Christ is our focus we can ignore the flesh and receive His provision of everything we need to produce Spiritual fruit (2 Peter 1:3-4, Hebrews 13:20-21, Philippians 2:3, Deuteronomy 30:11-14, Ephesians 2:10).

We have been created anew in Christ. We now have a Spiritual nature. We are righteous because of what He has done. When we identify with our flesh instead of His righteousness, we will wallow in the dust of the flesh. We cannot overcome the thorn of the flesh without the Word. His Divine influence is enough to defeat the enemy *when* we use it. It will raise up the barrier and ward off the flesh if we will remain in our proper position. We must see ourselves in

Christ; He must be our focus and our Divine influence. We must recognize who we are, whose we are, and what is rightfully ours.

> Isaiah 31:4 KJV For thus hath the LORD spoken unto me, Like as the lion and the young lion roaring on his prey, when a multitude of shepherds is called forth against him, he will not be afraid of their voice, nor abase himself for the noise of them: so shall the LORD of hosts come down to fight for mount Zion, and for the hill thereof.

Who am I? I am the young lion standing with *the* Lion of the tribe of Judah (Revelation 5:5). I am with Him and I am standing up over defeated prey. The enemy is defeated when I am in the presence of Christ - whether I can see it or not! The enemy can still make noise, but I do not have to listen. My Savior is the Lion, the enemy tries to imitate Him but there is no comparison (1 Peter 5:8). He may roar and voice his lies but when I am in my Savior's presence I will not fear. I will see the lies for what they are. I will not abase myself because of his noise when I am focused on Christ.

What does it mean to abase yourself? We discover that abase is a sadistic, injurious word when we look at the

Hebrew meaning. This word describes self-deprecation. When we listen to the lies of the enemy we are hurting ourselves. We depress ourselves, we deal harshly with ourselves, we trouble ourselves - we make ourselves miserable when we listen to the lies of the enemy. We do not have to hurt ourselves any longer! We are children of God. We are the young lions standing with Jesus. Now we are in His presence and now we have His righteousness and His power.

Are there lies coming against you? The Word is sufficient. It will raise up the barrier you need. It will protect you from the lies and give you the power to rebel against them.

> Isaiah 54:17 KJV "No weapon that is formed against thee shall prosper; and every tongue that shall rise against thee in judgment thou shalt condemn. This is the heritage of the servants of the LORD, and their righteousness is of Me," saith the LORD.

The lies that come against you are the weapon of the enemy. His voice or tongue is nothing more than evil babbling. The enemy spews this weapon of evil babbling in an attempt to get close to you and invade your space, but in judgment you can condemn this weapon.

The word translated as judgment is defined as a verdict and a privilege. God's final verdict for the life of the Christian is favorable! His good promises are the privilege of every believer. His verdict for your life is every single one of His promises. Using His great and precious promises, you can condemn the evil babbling of the enemy. When the lies of the enemy rise up, you need to rise up. Do not let his caustic lies become your dwelling place. Condemn the lies. This Biblical word "condemn" is defined as something disruptive and destructive. God's judgment (His Promises) will disturb the lies of the enemy and it will publically denounce them. When you rise up and roar you are looking down on the lie and magnifying the truth. You are declaring the truth and thereby announcing the termination of the lie. This is your right as God's dearly loved child. You have the right to speak the true promises of God and watch the enemy flee at the sound of your God's voice (Isaiah 33:3).

The lies of the enemy are no place for you to call home. It is time for the children of God to rise up and depart from the lies of the enemy. His lies are impure, they are destructive, and they are not your place of rest. When we are engaging with the lies of the enemy we will live in anxiety, fear, doubt, condemnation, and stress - just to name a few. Why do we do this to ourselves? Why do we abase ourselves?

Why do we make ourselves miserable?

I am not sure what your answer is to the question of why, I am not even completely sure what my answer is, but I do know it is rooted in giving lies preeminence. I also know that it is time to make a lasting change. The answer for abasing ourselves is the Word of God. It is time to arise and depart from the flesh and walk in His truth, His righteousness. I am His dearly loved child. His promises are my heritage and my righteousness is from Him. I have Jesus Christ on my side. He is my advocate. Why would I want to continue to ignore His love for me?

Many times we ignore the truth of His love because we do not feel worthy, but again, that is simply the result of improper focus and the acceptance of misinformation. When we are in the spotlight Christ cannot be. It will be impossible to see myself in Christ when I am so focused on what I do and don't do. If you are struggling with your focus, then look to the Word. Study verses about who you are in Christ. Focus on the truth and the lies will not be able to survive. Memorize the truth of the Word, think about it, speak it. We can escape the lies but we can only do so through the Word. It is our only advantage over the lies.

The Word is sufficient. It serves to transform us. It is useful and advantageous. We need it. Paul was happy to receive it because he understood how weak he was on his own. He didn't let that weakness get him down. He was happy to admit he was weak because that meant that Christ's power had a home in his life. When we think we are powerful on our own, we will not be able to receive His power. The Word will not be to our advantage. The Bible tells us that the poor in Spirit are blessed for this very reason (Matthew 5:3). Those who realize they are Spiritually bankrupt apart from Christ can receive every good thing that is available to them. They can participate in their new nature and receive from Christ because they are not full of self. We are our own obstacle when it comes to kingdom living when we live focused on what we assume we can do for God. Spiritually we have nothing to offer God, but He has everything to offer to us. We will begin to receive when we see things this way. His Word will be profitable in your life when you realize how desperate you are for it. The Word works. It will take the poor in Spirit and give them the riches of the Kingdom of God!

Are you receiving? Are you living the life of the young lion? We see that the young lion does not just ignore the lies of the enemy but he also roars. This word was translated from the Hebrew word *hagah* and its definition is a descriptive process. This word is a portrayal of the child of

God who studies the Word, ponders the Word, meditates on the Word, and speaks the Word. We receive sufficiently when this process is being worked out in our own lives. The Word is alive! It is in you, child of God - work it out of you! Your trial is an opportunity to feed on the Word - and what goes in will come out. As you study the Word and think about the Word, your words will begin to line up with the promises of God. Some days you may hear their faint whisper and other days you may hear them roar - no matter how loud the voice of the Word is in your life, you need to continue to fill yourself with it. The enemy is always trying to voice his opinion and we must have God's promises to combat the lies. We must be rooted in the truth of His love letter to us.

Chapter 11

1 Approve This Message

Haggai 1:13 KJV

Then spake Haggai the Lord's messenger in

the Lord's message unto the people, saying,

"I am with you," saith the Lord.

During election season we often hear and see ads posted by candidates. A famous line at the end of each of these ads boasts, "My name is ___________ and I approve this message." What does it mean to approve a message? It means that we agree with it or we support it. I would like to ask each of you, "What is your name and what message are you approving today?"

A message is defined by several definitions but in Webster's Dictionary I believe we find the most relevant definition: an underlying theme or idea. Underlying - the sometimes latent but significant premise or suggestion. It is essential and therefore very important. A message is designed to influence us. It is something communicated to us with the mission to sway us one way or another.

Some messages are very obvious. For example, many times we hear (audibly or wordlessly) that if we don't do *this*, then *that* will happen. If we don't agree with the crowd, we will be rejected. If we don't wear the latest designer fashions, we cannot be stylish. If we don't do what someone else wants us to do, consequences will follow.

These messages are sent in various ways but they have the same objective: to get us to do what someone else wants us to do. These messages are sent with the assignment of letting you know that you must do what someone else wants you to do or else. These messages can be bold and they are often rude. The messages are sent to control you because if you can control someone's mind, then you can essentially control their lives. The world understand this and that is why we are consistently bombarded with messages. As Christians, we need to understand this so that we can fight back with the truth of the Word of God.

These palpable messages will mostly likely affect us in one of two ways: we will boldly disapprove the message in an effort to rebel against the message or we will silently be influenced and led in a direction we do not necessarily agree with. If we have a Spiritually strong mind, we will be able to think based on the Word and the Word alone, but most of us need to work on strengthening our minds so that we will not be swayed in the wrong direction.

Some messages are subtle. For example, the passing billboard of a supermodel that makes us feel insecure or the disapproving look we get from someone we look up to when we do not agree with them. These subtle messages do not lack in power when compared to the obvious ones, at times they are even more powerful.

My amazing son has a master's degree and he continues to study the mind. I am not as educated as he is in the matters of the mind, but I have learned a lot from him, and more importantly, from the Word of God. The mind directs the course of our lives and it needs to be treated accordingly. We cannot give just any old thought permission to take up space in our minds. Our minds are priceless and precious and we need to understand what we are doing when we let thoughts that disagree with the Word take up residence in our minds. Thoughts matter. They are vital. The old adage, "It's the thought that counts," may not apply when it comes to actions, but it certainly does apply when it comes to life.

The Word of God is the message we should be approving in our lives. The Word of God is truth. The Word is the message we should seek to fill ourselves with as

Christians. Jesus told us that abiding in the Word leads to a knowledge of the truth and that the truth will consequently set us free (John 8:31-32). We need to live out those verses in our daily lives.

The messages of the world can only be silenced by the truth of the Word. The Word and its Divine influence in our lives is sufficient. It's the one thing that will take care of everything. The Word will defeat the lies in your life. When we know who we are in Christ, truth will reign and we will live in the freedom only Christ can give.

Every day countless messages are either approved or rejected by us. Haggai spoke the Lord's message to the people and it was simply, "I am with you." What a life-transforming message from our loving, heavenly Father. He is with us. We are not alone. We are not helpless. We have the Creator of the universe with us. Do we approve this message?

Do we live our lives as if God Almighty is with us or do we go it alone in hopes of getting by? We were created for so much more. Christ in you is your hope of glory; He is all you need to live life to the fullest as God intended (Colossians 1:27). As we approve the message of, "God is with us," we will manifest His glory and goodness. If you find it difficult to agree with this message that God is with you, then you are in need of the Word on this subject. Find as many verses as you can that declare this truth and surround yourself with them. We need to be in agreement with God rather than the enemy.

In the book of Nehemiah we see the enemy coming against God's children with a false message. He is assaulting them with lies. Nehemiah's response can inspire us.

> Nehemiah 6:8-9 NIV I sent him this reply: "Nothing like what you are saying is happening; you are just making it up out of your head." They were all trying to frighten us, thinking, "Their hands will get too weak for the work, and it will not be completed." But I prayed, "Now strengthen my hands."

The lies of the enemy are voiced in an effort to scare us. Nehemiah was aware of this and he fought back. We can learn a lot from this. Fear is paralyzing; it weakens us. Fear has this power to degrade because it is of the flesh. It is not Spiritual; therefore, nothing good can come from it. Nehemiah knew this truth and he didn't put up with the lies of the enemy. He roared! He declared loud and clear that the threats of the enemy were invalid and he announced the termination of the lie by speaking the truth of the Word and he continued to seek strengthening truth from His God. God's verdict for his life was greater than the lie and Nehemiah knew it. We can defy the power of the lie when we are walking in our Spiritual nature because we have the authority Christ gave us.

> 2 Kings 18:7 KJV And the LORD was with him; and he prospered whithersoever he went forth: and he rebelled against the king of Assyria, and served him not.

Hezekiah, like Nehemiah, was able to rebel against the enemy because God was with him and we can do likewise. Don't forget the message of the Lord. He is with us. We are His dearly loved children and because of this, we do not have to live in bondage to our flesh. We can rebel. To rebel means to fight back and refuse to conform. When we rebel we let the enemy know that he has no authority in our lives because Jesus Christ gave us His authority (Luke 10:19). And remember, your enemy is anything that disagrees with the Word of God. We do not fight against flesh and blood (Ephesians 6:12). We are in a war with anything that contradicts the Word of God, not people.

Hezekiah did not serve the enemy and we do not have to either. We do not have to live as a slave to our flesh. The messages of the flesh are self-defeating. "You can't change. That's just the way you are. It runs in your family. God could never forgive you. You've gone too far." We have all heard these messages and so many more but what we do with them is what matters. Hezekiah wasn't a slave to the lies, neither was Nehemiah. They found freedom in the truth of God's good promises and you can too!

The Lord is with you! Rebel! Fight back against the lies that are trying to paralyze you by focusing on Jesus Christ. Refuse to conform. It is your right as a dearly loved child of God. Your name is dearly loved child of God and you approve the message of God's love letter to you! Abide in His Word, dearly loved child of God, and live under His Divine influence today!

An off-season is a dry time in life. It is a time of lack – a lack of progress, a lack of success, a lack of victory. It involves trials and feelings of loneliness. During an off-season you may feel like God is not listening to you; you may even feel like He does not care about your struggle or your pain. This feeling is not based on the truth of God's Word and it will lead to more problems and negativity. Off-Season is an in-depth study focused on God's love for you and His plan for your off-seasons.

https://whitestephanie83.wixsite.com/heavenonearthforyou

More books by Stephanie White

Heaven on Earth: it is a life most people believe is not possible to achieve, but according to God's Word that is exactly what we can have! Heaven on Earth takes you on a journey through the Word of God so that you can find out what is available to you as God's child and you will also discover how to enjoy this life to the fullest.

In God's Word we discover that we are to live by faith, but we also see that faith is a fight. As a Christian, faith is essential. Eternal value is assigned to our faith. This book is an in-depth study of faith - what faith is, how we obtain it, how it works, what classifies it as genuine, what its benefits are, and more.

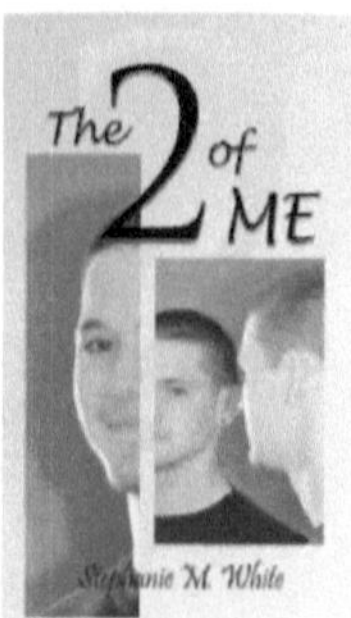

As Christians, we must understand that we have two natures - our Spiritual nature and our flesh. Each nature wants to dominate, but only one can. This book will take you through a thorough study of your two natures and it will help you understand each one. It will also show you how to rule over your flesh and defeat its power in your life.

https://whitestephanie83.wixsite.com/heavenonearthforyou

WORDS OF LIFE DEVOTIONALS
by Stephanie White and Kathleen Higham:

Available now!

SUMMER EDITION   **FALL EDITION**   **WINTER EDITION**

Each daily devotional is a ninety-day journey through the Word of God.

Coming Soon

https://whitestephanie83.wixsite.com/heavenonearthforyou

A Season of Grief

is a unique devotional designed to facilitate those who have suffered loss and are grieving.

Grief can bring even the strongest to their knees. As we endure a season of grief we will experience a myriad of emotions that we cannot ignore. As you read through this devotional you will find encouragement to deal with these feelings and move forward in spite of them because you are abiding in the Word of God.

We must invite Christ into our season of grief; we must take in His Word and receive the healing that only He can provide.

Our loved ones who have gone on ahead of us want us to enjoy the life that we have left; they want us to remember them and smile and look forward to being reunited with them.

The Word of God is our life. It is meant to be our daily life. This devotional will help you incorporate the Word of God into your life even as you press past the pain of loss.

WORDS OF LIFE DEVOTIONAL ~ A SEASON OF GRIEF EDITION

https://whitestephanie83.wixsite.com/heavenonearthforyou